Everyday Thai
for Beginners

Wiworn Kesavatana-Dohrs, Ph.D

Illustrated by Mary Ellen Dohrs

SILKWORM BOOKS

Everyday Thai for Beginners

© 2007 by Wiworn Kesavatana-Dohrs, Ph.D

ISBN 978-974-9575-97-0

First published in 2007 by Silkworm Books

6 Sukkasem Road, Suthep
Chiang Mai 50200 Thailand
E-mail address: info@silkwormbooks.com
http://www.silkwormbooks.com

Printed in Thailand by O. S. Printing House, Bangkok

Contents

Introduction

Everyday Thai for Beginners has been developed for students in Beginning Thai classes at the University of Washington. It is the product of many years of frustration of trying to teach students to speak Thai outside Thailand. After seeing the quality of materials for ESL (English as a Second Language) students, this book was written to provide a framework for students to use Thai interactively and communicatively through the use of games and various activities suggested in the book. It is not a teacher-based teaching method. Therefore it is suitable to be used in classes with large numbers of students.

This book is neither comprehensive nor perfect. Because of its size and scope, the book cannot possibly cover the wide range of regional variations and colloquialisms used in Thailand. It is meant to provide an introduction to the basics of communication using Central Thai vocabulary and idioms. Teachers using this book should be prepared to provide supplementary materials and concepts, appropriate to the needs of their particular students. In my teaching practice I often use contemporary, real-world materials as supplements, including newpapers, advertisement, flyers, coupons and so forth, to bring real life into the classroom.

This book has been used at the University of Washington for eight years and students' spoken ability has been quite gratifying. There are a total of seven units and thirty thematic lessons, each consisting of selected vocabulary items, simple sentence patterns, grammar, drills, suggested activities, written exercises, and cultural information. Grammar sections explain the important sentence patterns, which, if mastered, will give a solid foundation for students' spoken abilities. However, the main purpose of this book is to teach students to speak Thai, rather than to focus on grammatical or linguistic explanations.

Unlike most Thai language texts, this book does not use any transliteration. One must learn how to read and write prior to using this book. Based on my experience of teaching Thai for more than fifteen years, students who study Thai in Thai have far better pronunciation and tones than students who learn Thai phonetically. Suggestions on how to teach the Thai writing system are also included in this book in the section, "On the Thai Writing System." It should take about ten to fifteen hours to master the Thai writing system.

Everyday Thai for Beginners is designed for one year of academic Thai (30 weeks, 150 hours). After completing the book, students should be able to speak Thai at a survival level and read and write simple correspondence. The accompanying CDs are designed to be used with the book. Student should listen to the CDs until they understand the meaning and can reproduce the words and sentences without much effort. The CDs include the introductory chapter, "On the Thai Writing System," and the vocabulary, patterns, and drills in each chapter.

Thai people greatly appreciate foreigners who learn their language. Your study of Thai will be amply rewarded in Thailand.

Wiworn Kesavatana-Dohrs, Ph.D

Acknowledgments

There are several people who have made this project possible. The author would like to thank Dr. Mingquan Suksanong, Dr. Thawatchai Suksanong and Dr. Prapha Gajabhuti. Without them, I would not be where I am now. Special thanks to Mary Ellen Dohrs who has made this book more interesting and useful with her beautiful drawings; my husband, Larry Dohrs, who gave me support and encouragement and also proofread the manuscript.

Thanks also go to hundreds of my students who inspired me to write this book and who also served as guinea pigs, especially to Patrick McCormick for his suggestions and comments. My children, Marie (มาลี) and Jasper (เจตน์), also motivated me, being half Thai and growing up abroad, similar to many of my students. Knowledge of Thai language is the key to their understanding of their heritage.

This book is dedicated to my parents, Phithee and Prachathip Kesavatana, who provided me unconditional love, support, and encouragement.

On the Thai Writing System*

To understand how Thai is written, one needs to examine the language systematically. Non-Thai learners cannot learn it in the same way that Thai children study it. Below are suggestions on how to proceed, along with some examples. Assistance from an educated native speaker is essential because more examples and reading exercises need to be supplemented. Treat this only as a general guideline!

I. THAI TONES

Thai has five tones.

mid	(เสียงสามัญ)
low	(เสียงเอก)
falling	(เสียงโท)
high	(เสียงตรี)
and rising	(เสียงจัตวา)

An example of each with its transcribed symbol is given below.

mid	low	falling	high	rising
dii (ดี)	sii (สี่)	haa (ห้า)	naa (น้ำ)	sii (สี)

---

*This section is adapted from William Kuo, *A Workbook for Writing Thai*, Center for Southeast Asia studies, University of California, Berkeley: California, 1979.

II. THAI VOWELS

Thai has nine "short" vowels with their "long" counterparts.

Short vowels	Long vowels
อะ	อา
อิ	อี
อุ	อู
เอะ	เอ
แอะ	แอ
โอะ	โอ
เออะ	เออ
เอาะ	ออ
อึ	อือ

There are three diphthongs in Thai. They are:

เอีย (อี + อา)   อัว (อู + อา)   เอือ (อือ + อา)

(Their short counterparts, เอียะ, อัวะ, เอือะ, are not very common.)

There are four vowels that have a built in final consonant in their pronunciations. They are considered as "non-short vowels."

อำ   ไอ, ใอ   เอา   เอย

(Students must distinguish between short and non-short/long vowels since they produce different tones).

III. THAI CONSONANTS

1. Middle Class Consonants (อักษรกลาง)

There are nine middle class consonants in Thai.

ก   จ   ฎ   ฏ   ด   ต   บ   ป   อ

Tone Rules for Middle Class Consonants (MC)

1.1 MC + Non-Short Vowels = Mid Tone

e.g. กา, แจ, ไต, ใบ, เปีย, เอา, ดำ

1.2 MC + Short Vowels = Low Tone

e.g. จะ, ติ, เกาะ, แปะ, บุ, ดุ, เออะ

1.3 MC + Final Consonants

There are only eight final consonant sounds (primary finals) in Thai: five sonorant finals and three stop finals.

Sonorant finals	ม	น	ย	ว	ง
Stop finals	ก	ด	บ		

There are seven vowels that change forms when a syllable has a final consonant. These seven are:

Initial consonant + vowel	Final consonant	Final forms-
กะ	บ	กับ
เปะ	น	เป็น
โจะ	ง	จง
ปือ	น	ปืน
เบอ	ก	เบิก
แดะ, เดะ	ก	แด็ก, เด็ก
ตัว	ง	ตวง

a. MC + Vowel + Sonorant Final = Mid Tone

e.g. ดม, กัน, จูง, ตาม, บน, เปีย, อัน

b. MC + Vowel + Stop Final = Low Tone

e.g. ดก, บาด, ออก, จัก, แปด, เจ็บ

1.4 MC and Tone Symbols

A tone symbol can also determine the tone of a syllable.

There are four tone symbols in Thai.

Symbols		Names
'	ไม้เอก	low tone mark
๒	ไม้โท	falling tone mark
๗	ไม้ตรี	high tone mark
+	ไม้จัตวา	rising tone mark

a. MC + Low Tone Mark = Low Tone

e.g. ไก่, เป้า, แก่, ด่า, เก่า, เตี่ย, บ่อ, แต่

b. MC + Falling Tone Mark = Falling Tone

e.g. เป้า, จี้, ตู้, เก้า, ได้, บ้า, บ้าน, อ้อม, ต้น

c. MC + High Tone Mark = High Tone

e.g. เจ๊, โต๊ะ, เบ๊ะ, เกี๊ยะ, แจ๊ว, เต๊ะ, เก๊, ก๊าบ

d. MC + Rising Tone Mark = Rising Tone

e.g. ตุ๋น, เก๋า, จ๋า, เก๋, ตั๋ว, ไก๋, อ๋อ, ตี๋, จ๋อ

2. High Class Consonants (HC) (อักษรสูง)

There are eleven high class consonants in Thai.

ข   ฃ   ฉ   ฐ   ถ   ผ   ฝ   ศ   ษ   ส   ห

(ฃ is an archaic high class consonant and may be ignored)

Tone Rules for High Class Consonants (HC)

2.1 HC + Non-Short Vowels = Rising Tone

e.g. ขา, ผี, สี, ไห, เสือ, โถ, ขำ, เฉา, แส, เฉีย, หอ

2.2 HC + Short Vowels = Low Tone

e.g. ฉะ, เผียะ, เหอะ, เฉะ, สุ, เสาะ, เผือะ, เสะ, โถะ

2.3 HC + Final Consonants

a. HC + Vowels + Sonorant Finals = Rising Tone

e.g. ผม, โหม, หิน, แผน, สาย, เฉย, ถัง, ผัง, ฉวย, เขย

b. HC + Vowels + Stop Finals = Low Tone

e.g. ฉก, เผือก, สาก, ฉอก, สูบ, สาบ, ถีบ, เถิด, สูด, ถัด

2.4 HC and Tone Symbols

Thai has five tones, but high class consonant syllables are restricted to only three tones, that is rising, low, and falling. Only two tone symbols are applicable to the high class consonant. They are the low tone mark and the falling tone mark.

a. HC + Low Tone Mark = Low Tone

    e.g. เข่า, สี่, แผ่, ใฝ่, เห่อ, ห่อ, ไข่, ผ่า, เสื่อ, เสี่ย

b. HC + High Tone Mark = Falling Tone

    e.g. ข้า, ให้, ฝ้า, ผู้, สู้, เข้า, เสื้อ, เข้, ผ้า, ถ้า, ไส้

3. Low Class Consonants (LC) (อักษรต่ำ)

There are twenty-four low class consonants in Thai.

ค	ต	ฆ	ช	ฌ	ซ	ฑ	ท	ธ	ฒ
ณ	น	พ	ภ	ฟ	ม	ย	ญ	ร	ล
ว	ฬ	ฮ							

(ต, ฆ and ฑ may be ignored; ฒ, ฟ is rare)

Tone Rules for Low Class Consonants (LC)

3.1   LC + Non-Short Vowels = Mid Tone

    e.g. คา, รือ, โท, ไฟ, เมา, นำ, วัว, เลีย, เท, ใย

3.2   LC + Short Vowels = High Tone

    e.g. คะ, แงะ, เลอะ, มุ, เคาะ, นะ, แทะ, แยะ

3.3   LC with Final Consonants

    a. LC + Vowel + Sonorant Finals = Mid Tone

    e.g. คม, ชืน, มวน, ยุง, พวง, พัง, นอน, เทียน, เลว

    b. LC +Non-Short Vowels + Stop Finals = Falling Tone

    e.g. ซีก, แลก, มาก, ชอบ, ยาก, เลิก, มืด, พูด, รีบ, ยอด

    c. LC + Short Vowels + Stop Finals = High Tone

    e.g. ซัก, รัด, ทับ, คบ, มด, ทุก, พัก, ชุก, ลุก, พัด, เล็บ

3.4   LC with Tone Symbols

Only two tone symbols (ไม้เอก, ไม้โท) are applicable to low class consonants. Low class consonants are restricted to three tone sounds—mid, low, and falling.

a. LC + Low Tone Mark = Falling Tone

e.g. ค่า, นี่, ชั่ว, พ่อ, แม่, ชื่อ, น่า, ทู่, แช่, แน่

b. LC + Falling Tone Mark = High Tone

e.g. นี้, ม้า, รื้อ, ไม้, ใช้, ค้า, ชื้อ, ช้า, น้ำ, ล้อ

Low Class Consonants: Special Feature

1. A *silent* ห may precede some low class consonants. These low class consonants are below.

ง   น   ม   ญ   ย   ร   ล   ว

These low class consonants are called **อักษรเดี่ยว**, which means that they do not have high consonant counterparts. Some low class consonants have high consonant counterparts which are called **อักษรคู่** e.g. **ค/ข, ช/ฉ, ท/ถ, ฟ/ฝ, ซ/ส, ศ, ษ** etc. Low class consonants with *silent* ห in front will be pronounced as if they are high class syllables, taking high class tone characteristics.

e.g. หมา, เหล่า, หงาย, หยุด, หญิง, หน้า, หนาม, หน่าย

2. There are four instances when a *silent* อ precedes the low class consonant ย. These syllables will take middle class tone characteristics.

อย่า	(do not)	อยู่	(to be located at)
อยาก	(to want)	อย่าง	(type, kind)

Secondary Final Consonants

Thai has only eight final consonant sounds, as mentioned earlier, but some other letters may appear as final consonants. These are called secondary finals. When they occur, they have to be pronounced as one of the primary finals.

Primary Finals	Secondary Finals	Example
น	ณ, ญ, ล, ร	คุณ, การ, โบราณ
ก	ค, ข, ฆ	โรค, เมฆ
บ	ป, พ, ภ	บาป, โลภ, เทพ

Primary Finals	Secondary Finals	Example
ด	ช, ต, จ	ราช, วัตถุ, อาจ
	ถ, ท, ธ, ฐ	อาพาธ, บทบาท, รัฐ
	ส, ศ, ษ	โอกาส, กระดาษ, ดาบส
	ฏ, ฎ	กฏ

Consonant Clusters

There are thirteen consonant clusters in Thai. The tone of the consonant cluster syllable is determined by the class of the first consonant of the cluster. If there is a tone symbol, it is placed over the second consonant.

ปร   ปล   ตร   กร   กล   กว   พร   พล   คร   คล   คว

Polysyllabic Words

If the initial syllable of a polysyllabic word is either a middle class or high class consonant plus an unwritten ะ, and the second syllable is low class consonant, the low class consonant will take the tone characteristics of the initial consonant.

e.g. จมูก, ขนม, ตลาด, สนุก, ถนน, ตลอด, ขนาด, ฉลาด

Special Cases

There are seven particular features in the writing system.

1. ทร is read as ซ when ทร are initial consonants.

   e.g. ทราบ, ทราย, ทรง, ทราม

2. In some cases, ร is not pronounced.

   e.g. จริง, สร้าง, สระ, เสริม, เศร้า, สามารถ

3. Double รร is pronounced as อะ, unless followed by a final, in which case it is pronounced as อัน.

   e.g. สรร, กรรม, บรรพ, กรรไกร

4. In some rare cases, you'll find two consonants in which the second one is ร with no vowel/final consonant. ร should be pronounced as ออน.

   e.g. กร, นคร, บังอร, อาทร

7

5. The symbol ๆ which is called ไม้ยมก, means that the word should be read twice.

   e.g. เร็วๆ, ดีๆ, เผ็ดๆ, เด็กๆ

6. The symbol ◌์ , which is called การันต์ will silence the letter that appears beneath it.

   e.g. อาจารย์, กีตาร์, โพธิ์, องค์

7. The symbol ฤ is pronounced รึ; ริ, เรอะ, ฤๅ are pronounced รือ.

   e.g. อังกฤษ, ฤดู, ฤกษ์, ฤทธิ์

Lesson 1: What Is This Called?

((●)) คำศัพท์

PRONOUNS

นี่	this	คุณ	you

NOUNS

ปากกา (ด้าม)	pen	หนังสือ (เล่ม)	book
ดินสอ (แท่ง)	pencil	ภาษา (ภาษา)	language
สมุด (เล่ม)	notebook	ภาษาไทย	Thai language

*Words in parentheses are classifiers.

VERBS

เรียกว่า	to call	สวย	to be beautiful
คือ	to be	แพง	to be expensive
พูด	to say	ถูก	to be cheap
เข้าใจ	to understand	ยาก	to be difficult
มี	to have	ง่าย	to be easy
ร้อน	to be hot (temperature)	ชอบ	to like
เผ็ด	to be spicy hot	ดี	to be good
อร่อย	to be delicious	เอา	to take, to want
สนุก	to have fun, to be enjoyable		

QUESTION WORDS

อะไร	what	อย่างไร, ยังไง	how
ใคร	who		

POLITE PARTICLES

คะ, ค่ะ, ครับ

PATTERNS

นี่ อะไร คะ/ครับ	What is this?
(นี่) ปากกา ค่ะ/ครับ	A pen.
(นี่) ดินสอ ค่ะ/ครับ	A pencil.

นี่ เรียก ว่า อะไร คะ/ครับ	What is this called?
หนังสือ ค่ะ/ครับ	A book.
เรียกว่า หนังสือ ค่ะ/ครับ	(It is) called a book.
นี่ เรียก ว่า หนังสือ ค่ะ/ครับ	It is called a book.

นี่ ภาษาไทย เรียกว่าอะไร คะ/ครับ	What is this called in Thai?
เรียก ว่า สมุด ค่ะ/ครับ	(It is) called a notebook.

Delicious ภาษาไทยพูดว่ายังไง	How do you say "delicious" in Thai?
Delicious ภาษาไทยพูดว่า อร่อย	It's "*aroi*" in Thai.

GRAMMAR

1. นี่ + คือ + อะไร What is this called?

The sentence pattern used when asking for words is นี่ + คือ + อะไร, คือ is equivalent to the verb "be" in English. In this pattern, the verb คือ is often omitted, except in formal writing. Unlike other verbs in Thai, คือ cannot have a negative form. To say, "This is not a pen," ไม่ใช่ is used for the negative form as in the pattern below.

e.g. นี่ ไม่ใช่ ปากกา   This is not a pen.
นี่ ดินสอ   It is a pencil.

To answer the นี่อะไร question, นี่ is omitted as Thais are likely not to repeat information that is mutually understood by both the speaker and the listener.

e.g. นี่อะไร   What is this?
(นี่) ปากกา   (It is) a pen.

2. S + V + O pattern

Thai follows the **S + V + O** word order. There is no requirement for Subject-Verb agreement in Thai. A question word remains in the position where it is substituted by the answer word. This rule is true of all question words. It is easy to think of it as substitution rule. Study the examples below.

	Subject	**Verb**	**Object**
Question	ใคร	ชอบ	คุณ
	Who likes you?		
Answer	เขา	ชอบ	ฉัน
	He likes me.		
Question	คุณ	ชอบ	ใคร
	Whom do you like?		
Answer	ฉัน	ชอบ	เขา
	I like him.		
Question	ใคร	มี	ปากกา
	Who has a pen?		
Answer	คุณ	มี	ปากกา
	You have a pen.		
Question	คุณ	มี	อะไร
	What do you have?		
Answer	ฉัน	มี	ปากกา
	I have a pen.		

3. English loan words

The verbs listed in the vocabulary section, e.g. **อร่อย, ดี, สวย, ชอบ, สนุก**, etc., are some of the most common verbs in Thai. There are also many English loan words in Thai that you can begin using. Below are some of them.

motorcycle	tissue	beer	style
jacket	taxi	wine	fashion
necktie	tour	hot dog	classic
sofa	shampoo	check	menu
computer	dictionary	bonus	free
TV	air-condition	coupon	alcohol
apartment	cookie	party	check-out
video	cake	resort	technology
cassette tape	ice cream	fan (boyfriend/girlfriend/spouse)	
CD	pie	credit	

e.g.   คุณชอบไอติมไหม
ปาร์ตี้สนุกไหม
คุณมีแชมพูไหม
เขามีแฟนไหม

4. Classroom expressions

ฟังนะ	Listen to me.
พูดตามอาจารย์	Repeat after me.
พูดอีกที	Say it again.
พูดถูกแล้ว	You said it correctly.
เก่งมาก	Very good.
เข้าใจไหม	Do you understand?

((•))) **DRILL**

1. "you"   ภาษาไทยพูดว่าอะไร
2. "to call"   ภาษาไทยพูดว่าอะไร
3. "to be delicious" ภาษาไทยพูดว่ายังไง
4. "to have"   ภาษาไทยพูดว่ายังไง
5. "to like"   ภาษาไทยพูดว่าอะไร
6. "to be good"   ภาษาไทยพูดว่าอะไร
7. "to be beautiful" ภาษาไทยพูดว่ายังไง
8. "to be spicy hot" ภาษาไทยพูดว่ายังไง
9. "to be expensive" ภาษาไทยพูดว่ายังไง
10. "to be hot"   ภาษาไทยพูดว่ายังไง
11. "a pen"   ภาษาไทยเรียกว่ายังไง
12. "a pencil"   ภาษาไทยเรียกว่ายังไง

CULTURAL CORNER

It is important in Thai culture to show courtesy toward other people, especially those who are older or in higher social or professional positions. Children are taught to speak politely once they learn how to talk. One's manner of speaking reflects one's upbringing, social background, and education.

One way to show courtesy toward others is the use of a polite particle in one's speech. The particle is placed at the end of a sentence. Following are the two sets of particles used by male and female speakers.

	Male speakers	**Female speakers**
Question	ครับ	คะ
Regular statement	ครับ	ค่ะ

Informal polite particles ฮะ, and จ๊ะ, จ๋ะ can also be used. ฮะ can be used by both males and females. จ๊ะ, จ๋ะ are used primarily by females and are used among friends or in informal situations. คะ, ค่ะ, ครับ sometimes are not used among friends. Remember to use these particles when you actually say the sentences in this book.

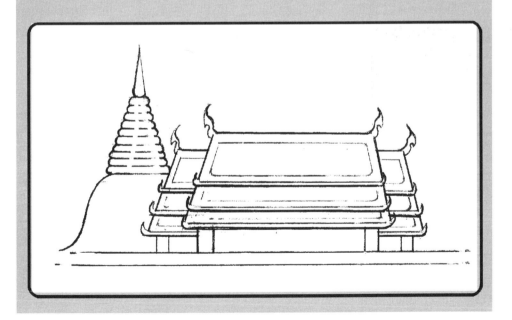

Unit 1
Getting to Know Each Other

Lesson 2: Hellos and Goodbyes

 คำศัพท์

GREETING

สวัสดี	hello

PRONOUNS

ดิฉัน	I (female)	เธอ	she, you	ท่าน	you, he, she
ผม	I (male)	เขา	he, she, they		
ฉัน	I	เรา	we, I		

NOUNS

ชื่อ (ชื่อ)	name, to be named
นามสกุล (นามสกุล)	surname, last name
ชื่อเล่น (ชื่อ)	nickname
โชค	luck

*Words in parentheses are classifiers.

VERBS

เป็น	to be	สบายดี	to be well, fine
ขอบคุณ	to thank, thank you	พบ, เจอ	to meet
ไป	to go	กลับ	to return
ลา	to say goodbye, to take leave		

NEGATIVE

ไม่	no, not	ไม่.....เลย	not at all

QUESTION WORDS

ใช่ไหม	tag question, right?	ไหม/มั๊ย	yes/no question word
หรือ/เหรอ/รึ	right?	แล้ว.....ล่ะ	what about.....

MISC.

V + กัน	V + each other	ใหม่	again, new
มาก	very	อีก	again
วันหลัง	later (a day in the future)		
ก่อน	first, before		
ลาก่อน	farewell		

PATTERNS: WHAT IS YOUR NAME?

สวัสดีค่ะ/ครับ	Hello.
คุณ ชื่อ อะไร คะ/ครับ	What is your name?
นามสกุล อะไร คะ/ครับ	What is your last name?
ดิฉัน ชื่อ..... นามสกุล..... ค่ะ	My name is..... (and my) last name is.....
ผม ชื่อ..... นามสกุล..... ครับ	

คุณ ชื่อ เอ ใช่ไหมคะ/ครับ	Your name is A, isn't it?
ใช่ค่ะ/ครับ	Yes.
ไม่ใช่ค่ะ/ครับ (ผม/ดิฉัน) ชื่อ บี	No, my name is B, not A.
ไม่ได้ชื่อ เอ	

เธอมีชื่อเล่น ไหม	Do you have a nickname?
มี	Yes, I do.
ไม่มี	No, I don't.
แล้ว เธอ ล่ะ	What about you?
ฉันมีชื่อเล่นว่า บี	My nickname is B.

PATTERN: INTRODUCTION

นี่ คุณ.....ค่ะ/ครับ

This is Mr./Mrs. .....

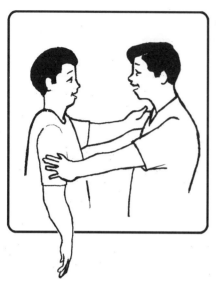

 PATTERNS: HELLOS

สวัสดีค่ะ/ครับ สบายดีหรือ (formal)

Hello. How are you?

    สบายดีค่ะ/ครับ ขอบคุณ แล้วคุณล่ะ

    I'm fine, thank you. What about you?

    สบายดีค่ะ/ครับ

    I'm fine.

เป็นไง (ยังไง) สบายดีหรือ/เหรอ (informal)

Hi. How are you?

เป็นยังไง ไปไหนมา (very informal, used

    among friends)

Hi. Where have you been?

 PATTERNS: GOODBYES

ไปก่อนนะ	I'm going.
ไปละนะ	I'm going.
ลาละนะ	Goodbye.
กลับก่อนนะ	I'm going home.
แล้วเจอกันใหม่	We'll see each other again.
แล้วพบกันใหม่	We'll see each other again.
แล้วพบกันอีก	We'll see each other again.
แล้วพบกันวันหลัง	We'll see each other later.
แล้วเจอกันวันหลัง	We'll see each other later.
โชคดี	Good luck.
ลาก่อน	Farewell.

GRAMMAR

1. อะไร what?

Unlike English, the question word อะไร does not necessarily begin the question. The question word will be where the answer would be (substitution rule). Substitute the answer for the question word อะไร when replying.

e.g. เขา ชื่อ อะไร   What is his/her name?

    เขา ชื่อ.....   His/her name is.....

คุณ นามสกุล อะไร	What is your last name (family name)?
ผม/ดิฉัน นามสกุล.....	My last name is.....

2. ไหม yes/no question word

ไหม is used to form simple yes/no questions such as "Is it good?" Just put ไหม at the end of a sentence. Answer "yes" by repeating the verb, or "no" by putting ไม่ before the verb.

e.g.	เขามีชื่อเล่นไหม	Does he/she have a nickname?
	Answer	มี (yes)
		ไม่มี (no)
	เอาไหม	Do you want (it)?
	Answer	เอา (yes)
		ไม่เอา (no)
	เข้าใจไหม	Do you understand?
	Answer	เข้าใจ (yes)
		ไม่เข้าใจ (no)
	ภาษาไทยยากไหม	Is Thai language difficult?
	Answer	ไม่ยากเลย ง่ายมาก (No, not difficult at all. It's very easy.)

In spoken language, ไหม is often pronounced as มั้ย. (Thai people have a tendency to change question words with rising tone sounds into high tone sounds.)

3. หรือ yes/no assumption question

หรือ is used to confirm one's idea. It is always placed at the end of a sentence.

e.g. เขาชื่อแดงหรือ His/her name is Daeng, right?

Answer	Yes:	ค่ะ/ครับ
	No:	ไม่ เขา ไม่ได้ ชื่อ แดง (Subj. + ไม่ได้ + Verb)

In spoken language, หรือ can be pronounced as รึ or เหรอ.

4. ใช่ไหม yes/no assumption tag question

Like หรือ, ใช่ไหม is used to ask a question that confirms one's understanding, e.g. "They live here, don't they?" ใช่ไหม always comes at the end of a sentence. To answer, use these patterns.

Question	Sentence + ใช่ไหม
Answer	Yes: ใช่
	No: ไม่ใช่ Subj. + ไม่ + VP (verb phrase)
	ไม่ใช่ Subj. + ไม่ได้ + VP

5. ไม่ได้

ไม่ได้ is used to correct misunderstandings posed in ใช่ไหม or หรือ questions. However, not all verbs can be used with ไม่ได้ such as มี, ชอบ, อยาก, อร่อย. In this case, use ไม่ + verb instead. Compare the examples below.

e.g. เขาชื่อทอมใช่ไหม His name is Tom, isn't it?

ไม่ใช่ เขาไม่ได้ชื่อทอม เขาชื่อทิม No, his name is not Tom. His name is Tim.

ทิม ชอบ ไอติม ใช่ไหม Tim likes ice cream, doesn't he?

ไม่ใช่ ทิม ไม่ ชอบ ไอติม No, he doesn't like ice cream.

6. แล้ว.....ล่ะ what about.....?

แล้ว.....ล่ะ is used when the question is already established so one does not have to repeat the whole question again.

e.g. คุณชื่ออะไร What is your name?

ชื่อแดง แล้วคุณล่ะ My name is Daeng. What about you?

คุณชอบไอติมไหม Do you like ice cream?

ชอบ แล้วคุณล่ะ Yes, I do. What about you?

7. มาก, ไม่.....เลย very, not at all

มาก or ไม่.....เลย can be used to answer a ไหม question instead of simply answering yes or no.

e.g. ผัดไทยอร่อยไหม Is *phad thai* delicious?

อร่อยมาก It's very good.

ไม่อร่อยเลย No, it's not good at all.

8. The use of pronouns in Thai

The use of pronouns in Thai is not as straightforward as it is in English. Thais often use names, occupations, or kinship terms as pronouns, which can be confusing to English speakers. Only the most common pronouns (คุณ, ดิฉัน, เขา, etc.) are used in this book in order to keep things simple. In fact, the choice of pronouns is very fluid and a speaker's actual choice conveys a lot of meaning, sometimes subtle and sometimes obvious. One needs to listen to daily use to learn how to use pronouns the Thai way.

Here is a brief description of how pronouns are used:

คุณ ("you" for both males and females) is very formal and therefore hardly used among friends. เธอ or friends' names are used instead of คุณ for both males and females. However, some husbands and wives use คุณ instead of names when referring to each other.

ดิฉัน ("I" for females) is very formal and not used among friends and acquaintances, as women tend to use names or kinship terms to refer to themselves. On some occasions, ดิฉัน is used with strangers or when kinship terms have not been established.

ฉัน ("I" for both males and females) is used among friends. Do not use ฉัน when talking to someone superior to yourself either in age or social/professional status. In spoken language, ฉัน is pronounced as ชั้น.

ผม ("I" for males) is more commonly used in both formal and informal situations. Its use is much less complicated than other pronouns.

เขา ("he," "she," "they" for both males and females) is pronounced as เค้า in spoken language. Names or kinship terms are often used instead of the pronoun เขา. พวกเขา or พวกเค้า is often used to mean "they." This chapter will use "he/she" to translate เขา. Subsequent chapters will alternate between English masculine and feminine forms for third person reference in Thai to avoid the cumbersome "he/she," although เขา is more commonly used for "he."

เธอ ("you" for males and females) is used instead of คุณ for both males and females. Be careful not to use it with persons who are "superior" in age or in social/professional status. It is acceptable to use with "inferior" persons. For example, a teacher can call a student เธอ whereas a student cannot call a teacher เธอ. เธอ can sometimes be used as a third-person pronoun for females only.

เรา can be used to mean "I," "you," or "we." Normally เรา is translated as "we" but it can also be used as the "royal I." Some people use เรา instead of ฉัน when talking to friends. เรา can also be used as "you" when speaking to "inferior" persons similar to เธอ, as mentioned earlier.

ท่าน ("you," "he," she") is used to show deference or respect. It is normally used with people of higher status than the speaker, both in age and in social status, or with monks. It can also be used as a title placed in front of names to show additional respect.

Besides the pronouns mentioned above, there are myriad informal pronouns that are used among friends, for example ข้า/เอ็ง, กู/มึง, etc. They are considered impolite but are used among close friends to show intimacy.

DRILL

1. เขาดีไหม	Is he/she a good person?
ดี	Yes.
ดีมาก	Yes, he/she is very good.
ไม่ดีเลย	No, he/she is not very good.
2. สวยไหม	Is it pretty? (yes, very beautiful)
3. แพงไหม	Is it expensive? (no, not at all)
4. สนุกไหม	Is it fun? (yes)
5. เอาไหม	Do you want it? (no)
6. ชอบไหม	Do you like it? (yes, very much)
7. ร้อนไหม	Are you hot? (yes, very much)
8. ดีไหม	Is it good? (no, not at all)

PARTNER ACTIVITIES

I. Introduce yourself to your partner, giving your first and last names. After that, introduce your partner to the class using this pattern.

เขา ชื่อ.....นามสกุล.....

II. Find different partners, asking each other your first and last names. Then introduce each other to the class using the pattern above.

CLASS ACTIVITY

Circulate around the room and greet each other.

สวัสดีค่ะ/ครับ เป็นยังไง สบายดีหรือ

สบายดีค่ะ/ครับ แล้วคุณล่ะ

สบายดีค่ะ/ครับ ขอบคุณ

FIND SOMEONE WHO . . .

Circulate around the classroom, using (affirmative) **ไหม** questions to ask your classmates questions and also their names to complete the exercise below. Practice asking questions with your teacher first.

e.g. คุณมีชื่อเล่นไหม; คุณชอบเบียร์ไหม

Find someone who . . .

.... has a nickname.

.... has a Thai name. (ชื่อไทย)

.... does not have a "fan." (แฟน, boyfriend/girlfriend)

.... does not have a TV.

EXERCISES

I. Match questions on the left with appropriate answers on the right.

1. Ice cream ภาษาไทยพูดว่ายังไง..... ก. สบายดีค่ะ ขอบคุณ แล้วคุณล่ะ

2. คุณชอบเบียร์ไหม..... ข. ไอติมสตอเบอรี่

3. เขาชื่อทอมใช่ไหม..... ค. ไม่อยากเลย

4. เป็นยังไง สบายดีหรือ..... ง. ชอบมาก

5. เขาไม่ชอบอะไร..... จ. ไม่ใช่ เขาชื่อดอน

6. คุณอยากมีแฟนไหม..... ฉ. ไอติม

7. ไปก่อนนะ..... ช. สวัสดี แล้วเจอกันใหม่

II. The conversation below is out of order. Please rewrite it in the space on the right or on a separate sheet of paper.

ก: สวัสดีค่ะ คุณชื่ออะไร

ข: สบายดีครับ แล้วคุณมาลีล่ะ

ก: ดิฉันชื่อมาลีค่ะ คุณมีชื่อเล่นไหม

ข: ผมชื่อทอม แล้วคุณล่ะ

ก: ดิฉันสบายดีค่ะ ขอบคุณ

ข: ไม่มีครับ

ก: คุณทอมสบายดีหรือคะ

CULTURAL CORNER

1. Thai people call each other by first names. Therefore when you ask someone's name, only the first name is usually given (ชื่อจริง, legal name, or ชื่อตัว, person's name). Thai people normally will not give their last names, unless asked specifically.

Most Thais have nicknames (ชื่อเล่น). Nicknames are used in informal situations or among friends and family. When asked for names, Thais might give you their nicknames instead of their legal names.

2. Thai people often omit a pronoun (subject) when it is already understood by both partners (speaker and listener). When a pronoun is necessary, Thais can also use names or kinship terms as pronouns. Study the examples.

ทอม:	แดงเป็นยังไง สบายดีหรือ	How are you, Daeng?
แดง:	สบายดี แล้วทอมล่ะ	I'm fine. What about you?
ทอม:	สบายดีครับ ขอบคุณ	I'm fine, thank you.

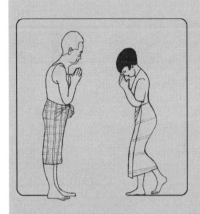

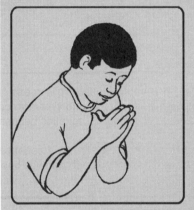

3. The *wai* is the Thai method of greeting. Thais do not shake hands, nor do they say "pleased to meet you" upon meeting. Some Thai people familiar with Western ways may say this to make a foreign visitor comfortable. But Thais do not say ยินดีที่ได้รู้จัก when they first meet.

As both Thai language and society are hierarchical, the *wai* serves as a physical illustration between the people greeting each other. The inferior" person (in age and in social/professional status) initiates the *wai*, and the greater the social distance between the parties, the more respectful the form of *wai* given. The receiver gives a less formal response.

Unequal status between individuals is determined by social position (monks always receive great respect), by age, and by authority. Determining status is often fluid. The best way is to look to your Thai friends for hints on the proper use of the *wai*.

The *wai* is used again upon taking leave. It is also used as a gesture of thanks and appreciation when someone gives you a gift or does you a favor. The same rules above apply to this *wai* as well.

Lesson 3: Where Are You From?

(((•))) **คำศัพท์**

NOUNS

ประเทศ (ประเทศ)	country	คน (คน)	person
จังหวัด (จังหวัด)	province	คน/ชาวต่างชาติ (คน)	foreigner
เมือง (เมือง)	country, city	เพื่อน (คน)	friend
ต่างจังหวัด (จังหวัด)	city outside Bangkok	ฝรั่ง (คน)	Westerner (Caucasian)
รัฐ (รัฐ)	state		
บ้าน (หลัง)	house		
โรงแรม (โรงแรม, แห่ง)	hotel		

*Words in parentheses are classifiers.

ที่นี่	here	ที่โน่น	that place over there
ที่นั่น	there		

VERBS

มา	to come	ขอโทษ	to excuse, excuse me
อยู่	to be (in location)	เป็น	to be
พัก	to stay		

PREPOSITIONS

จาก	from	ที่	at
กับ	with, and		

DEMONSTRATIVE ADJECTIVES

นี้	this	โน้น	over there
นั้น	that		

QUESTION WORDS

ไหน, ที่ไหน	where	ไหน	which

COUNTRIES

ประเทศกัมพูชา	Cambodia	ประเทศญี่ปุ่น	Japan
ประเทศจีน	China	ประเทศเกาหลี	Korea
ประเทศอังกฤษ	England	ประเทศพม่า	Myanmar
ประเทศฝรั่งเศส	France	ประเทศไทย	Thailand
ประเทศเยอรมัน	Germany	ประเทศสหรัฐ	U.S.A.

PATTERNS

ขอโทษค่ะ/ครับ คุณมาจากไหนคะ/ครับ — Excuse me. Where are you from?
ดิฉัน/ผมมาจาก ประเทศอเมริกาค่ะ/ครับ — I'm from America.

คุณอยู่ที่ไหนคะ/ครับ — Where do you live?

บ้าน (คุณ) อยู่ไหน — Where is your home?
อยู่กรุงเทพ — (My house) is in Bangkok.
อยู่ต่างจังหวัด — (My house) is outside Bangkok.
อยู่จังหวัดเชียงใหม่ — (My house) is in Chiang Mai.

คุณมาจากรัฐไหน — Which state are you from?
รัฐวอชิงตัน — (I'm from) Washington State.

คุณมาจากเมืองอะไร — What city are you from?
เมืองซีแอตเติล — (I'm from) Seattle.

คุณเป็นคนอเมริกันใช่ไหม — You are an American, aren't you?
ใช่ค่ะ/ครับ ดิฉัน/ผมเป็นคนอเมริกัน — Yes, I'm an American.
ไม่ใช่ค่ะ/ครับ ดิฉัน/ผมไม่ได้เป็นคน
อเมริกัน — No, I'm not an American.
ดิฉัน/ผมเป็นคนอังกฤษ — I'm English.

คุณพัก (อยู่) ที่ไหน — Where are you staying?
ดิฉัน/ผม พัก (อยู่) ที่โรงแรม — I am staying at a hotel.
ดิฉัน/ผม พัก (อยู่) ที่บ้านเพื่อน — I am staying at (my) friend's house.

คนนี้เป็นคนอเมริกันใช่ไหมคะ/ครับ	Is this person American?
ใช่ค่ะ/ครับ เขาเป็นคนอเมริกัน	Yes, he is an American.
เขาพักที่บ้านเพื่อนคนไหนคะ/ครับ	In which friend's house is he staying?
บ้านเพื่อนคนนี้ค่ะ/ครับ	(He is staying) at this friend's house.
บ้านเพื่อนคนไทยค่ะ/ครับ	(He is staying) at a Thai friend's house.
เขาพักกับเพื่อนคนไทยค่ะ/ครับ	He is staying with a Thai friend.

GRAMMAR

1. กับ with, and

a. To say, "I live with my mom and dad," or "I went to Thailand with my friends," use the pattern below.

S + V or VP + กับ + Object

ฉันอยู่กับพ่อแม่	I live with my mom and dad.
ฉันไปเมืองไทยกับเพื่อน	I went to Thailand with my friends.

b. To say, "I like Thai food and Chinese food," or "Thai food and Chinese food are delicious," use these patterns.

S + V + Object 1 + กับ/และ + Object 2
Subject 1 + กับ/และ + Subject 2 + V or VP

ฉันชอบอาหารไทยกับอาหารจีน	I like Thai food and Chinese food.
อาหารไทยกับ/และอาหารจีนอร่อย	Thai food and Chinese food are delicious.

2. ไหน which

ไหน is a question word for "which." It must be preceded by a classifier (clf). Do not confuse it with ไหน, which is also a short form of ที่ไหน (where) and does not need a classifier.

Noun + Clf + ไหน

e.g. เพื่อนคนไหนเป็นคนอเมริกัน	Which one of your friends is American?
เขาพักที่โรงแรมไหน	In which hotel is she staying?
เขาอยู่บ้านหลังไหน	In which house does she live?

3. นี้, นั้น, โน้น this, that, over there

Demonstrative adjectives นี้, นั้น, โน้น sometimes answer ไหน (which) questions. Substitute the answer for the question word (substitution rule) as in the examples below.

e.g.	เพื่อนคนนั้นเป็นคนอเมริกัน	That friend is American.
	เขาพักที่โรงแรมนี้	She is staying at this hotel.
	เขาอยู่บ้านหลังโน้น	She lives in that house over there.

As in no. 1, when using demonstrative adjectives นี้, นั้น, โน้น a classifier is a must. It is placed between a noun and a demonstrative adjective as in the examples below.

Noun + Clf + Dm. Adj

e.g.	บ้านหลังนี้	this house
	เพื่อนคนนั้น	that friend
	ประเทศนี้	this country
	จังหวัดนั้น	that province

Notice that when noun and classifier are identical (e.g. โรงแรม, ประเทศ, คน, จังหวัด), the noun is dropped. Also do not confuse this นี้ with the word นี่ from lesson 1. นี่ means "this" and is a pronoun, not an adjective, and therefore does not need a classifier.

4. ที่ไหน where

To ask a "where" question, use the question word ที่ไหน. Nouns ที่นี่ (here), ที่นั่น (there), ที่โน่น (that place over there) can be used to answer ที่ไหน questions.

e.g.	เขาอยู่ที่ไหน	Where does she live?
	เขาอยู่ที่นี่	She lives here.
	แล้วเพื่อนเขาล่ะ	What about her friend?
	เพื่อนเขาอยู่ที่นั่น	Her friend lives there.

DRILL

1. เขาเป็นคนไทยใช่ไหม (yes)
   He is Thai, isn't he?

2. เขาเป็นคนอเมริกันใช่ไหม (no)
   He is American, isn't he?

3. เขามาจากซีแอตเติลใช่ไหม (yes)
   He's from Seattle, isn't he?

4. เขาชื่อจอห์นใช่ไหม (no, his name is Jim)
   His name is John, isn't it?

5. เขาชื่อโจใช่ไหม (yes)
   His name is Joe, isn't it?

6. เขามาจากรัฐไหน (Oregon)
   From which state did he come?

7. เขามาจากเมืองอะไร (Bangkok)
   From which city did he come?

8. เขาพักที่โรงแรมไหน (this hotel)
   In which hotel did he stay?

9. คนไหนชื่อจิม (this person)
   Which person is Jim?

10. จิมอยู่ที่ไหน (here)
    Where is Jim?

((•)) SUBSTITUTION DRILLS

1. คุณ   มาจาก   ไหน
                        อเมริกา

   เขา
            อยู่
                        โรงแรม
                        เมืองไทย

            ชอบ
                        คนไหน
                        คนนี้

   ใคร

2. คุณ   ชอบ   อะไร
                        เมืองไทย

   คนนี้
            มา
                        บ้านเพื่อน

   เขา
            อยู่
                        โรงแรม

                                    ไหน (which)
                                    นี้

            ที่นี่

CLASS ACTIVITIES

I. Teacher makes as many cards as there are students. Each card contains a name and a country. Teacher distributes the identity cards to students. Students circulate around the classroom asking as many people as possible their names and where they are from.

ขอโทษนะคะ/ครับ คุณชื่ออะไรคะ/ครับ

    ดิฉัน/ผม ชื่อ ....

คุณมาจากไหนคะ/ครับ

    ดิฉัน/ผม มาจากประเทศ ....

II. Teacher makes a different set of cards containing only nationality and distributes them to students. Students circulate around the classroom trying to find as many people as possible with the same nationality using **ใช่ไหม** questions.

ขอโทษค่ะ/ครับ คุณเป็นคนไทยใช่ไหม

    ใช่ค่ะ/ครับ

    ไม่ใช่ค่ะ/ครับ ดิฉัน/ผมไม่ได้เป็นคนไทย

FIND SOMEONE WHO . . .

Circulate around the classroom, asking classmates **ไหม** questions to complete the exercise below.

    1............... ชอบเผ็ด

    2............... ไม่ชอบพิซซ่า

    3............... ไม่ชอบเบียร์

    4............... ไม่มีดินสอ

    5............... ไม่มีคอมพิวเตอร์

    6............... มีแฟน

Then teacher asks students questions to share the information they have found.

    e.g. ใครชอบเผ็ด etc.

PARTNER INTERVIEW

Practice these questions with your partner.

    1. คุณมาจากรัฐไหน or คุณมาจากไหน (originally)

    2. คุณมาจากเมืองอะไร

    3. บ้านคุณอยู่ที่ไหน (now)

Then report your findings to the classroom, using the pattern below.

คุณ.....มาจากเมือง.....รัฐ.....บ้านเขาอยู่ที่.....

GOSSIP GAME

Work in groups of eight. Choose a leader. The leader reads a secret passage given by the teacher, then whispers the secret to the student sitting next to him/her. The last student tells the secret to the class. Which group has the most accurate secret?

Alternatively, the teacher can whisper a secret to the leader who then passes it on to the next member of his group.

EXERCISES

I. Complete the conversation below.

มาลี : สวัสดีค่ะ   คุณชื่ออะไรคะ

ทอม : ....

มาลี : ดิฉันชื่อมาลี

ทอม : ....

มาลี : ดิฉันสบายดีค่ะ ขอบคุณ

ทอม : ....

มาลี : โชคดีค่ะ แล้วเจอกันวันหลัง

II. Read the following passage. Then answer the questions below in complete sentences.

โจเป็นคนอเมริกัน   มาจากเมืองซีแอตเติล   โจพักกับเพื่อนคนไทย
ไม่ได้พักที่โรงแรม   โจชอบเมืองไทยมาก

1. โจมาจากประเทศอะไร

2. เขาพักที่ไหน

3. โจพักที่โรงแรมใช่ไหม

4. เขาไม่ชอบเมืองไทยใช่ไหม

Lesson 4: How Old Are You?

 คำศัพท์

NUMBERS

๐	ศูนย์	zero	๑๒	สิบสอง	twelve
๑	หนึ่ง	one	๒๐	ยี่สิบ	twenty
๒	สอง	two	๒๑	ยี่สิบเอ็ด	twenty one
๓	สาม	three	๓๐	สามสิบ	thirty
๔	สี่	four	๔๐	สี่สิบ	forty
๕	ห้า	five	๕๐	ห้าสิบ	fifty
๖	หก	six	๖๐	หกสิบ	sixty
๗	เจ็ด	seven	๗๐	เจ็ดสิบ	seventy
๘	แปด	eight	๘๐	แปดสิบ	eighty
๙	เก้า	nine	๙๐	เก้าสิบ	ninety
๑๐	สิบ	ten	๑๐๐	หนึ่งร้อย	one hundred
๑๑	สิบเอ็ด	eleven			

.....พัน	.....thousand	.....แสน	.....hundred thousand
.....หมื่น	.....ten thousand	.....ล้าน	.....million

NOUNS

อายุ	age (in year)	อาหาร (ชนิด, อย่าง)	food
แฟน (คน)	boyfriend, girlfriend, spouse		
ลูก (คน)	child (offspring)	ธุรกิจ (ธุรกิจ)	business
ปี	year, year old		

*Words in parentheses are classifiers.

PRE-VERBS

เคย	to have ever (done something)
อยาก	to want to, would like to

VERBS

โสด	to be single	มาหา/ไปหา	to visit, to look for
แต่งงาน	to be married	ทำ	to do
เรียนหนังสือ	to study	เที่ยว	to go out and about
เก่ง	to be good at something	พูด	to speak, to talk
ทำงาน	to work	กิน/ทาน	to eat
		นาน	to be long (in time)

QUESTION WORDS

เท่าไร, เท่าไหร่	how much?
กี่	how many?
(แล้ว) หรือยัง	"already" or "not yet"?

MISC.

หลาย	several	V + ได้/ไม่ได้	can + V / can't + V
ครั้ง	times	ก็.....เหมือนกัน	also
แรก	the first	และ	and
จัง	very much (colloq.)	แต่	but
นิดหน่อย	a little bit	ครึ่ง	half

PATTERNS

ขอโทษค่ะ/ครับ คุณอายุเท่าไร	Excuse me. How old are you?
๒๐ ปีค่ะ/ครับ แล้วคุณล่ะ	(I'm) twenty years old. What about you?
๒๕ ปี ค่ะ/ครับ	I'm twenty-five years old.
คุณแต่งงานแล้วหรือยัง	Are you married (already or not yet)?
ค่ะ/ครับ ดิฉัน/ผมแต่งงานแล้ว	Yes, I'm (already) married.
ยังค่ะ/ครับ ดิฉัน/ผมเป็นโสด ยังไม่ได้	No, not yet. I'm single. (I'm) not yet
แต่งงาน	married.
คุณมีลูกกี่คน	How many children do you have?
มีลูกคนนึง	I have a child.
มีลูกหนึ่งคน	I have one child.
มีลูก ๒ คน	I have two children.
ยังไม่มีลูก	I do not have children yet.

คุณมีแฟนแล้วหรือยัง	Do you have a boyfriend/girlfriend (already)?
มีแล้วค่ะ/ครับ แต่ยังไม่ได้แต่งงาน	Yes, I do. But I'm not married yet.
ยังไม่มีค่ะ/ครับ	No, I don't (have one yet).
คุณอยากมีแฟนไหม	Would you like to have a boyfriend/girlfriend?
อยากค่ะ/ครับ	Yes, I would.
ไม่อยากค่ะ/ครับ	No, I wouldn't.
คุณชอบอาหารไทยไหม	Do you like Thai food?
ชอบมาก แล้วคุณล่ะ	Yes, very much. What about you?
ดิฉัน/ผมก็เหมือนกัน	I do too.
ดิฉัน/ผมชอบอาหารไทย แต่ไม่ชอบเผ็ด	I like Thai food but I don't like it spicy.
คุณชอบกินเผ็ดไหมคะ/ครับ	Do you like to eat spicy food?
ชอบค่ะ/ครับ แล้วคุณล่ะ	Yes, I do. What about you?
ดิฉัน/ผมก็ชอบกินเผ็ดเหมือนกัน	I like to eat spicy food also.
ดิฉัน/ผมไม่ชอบเผ็ดเลย	I don't like spicy (food) at all.
ดิฉัน/ผมกินเผ็ดไม่ได้	I cannot eat spicy food.
คุณเคยมาเมืองไทยกี่ครั้งแล้วคะ/ครับ	How many times have you been to Thailand (already)?
หลายครั้งแล้ว	Several times (already).
นี่เป็นครั้งแรก	This is the first time.
คุณมาทำอะไรที่เมืองไทย	What did you come to Thailand to do?
มาเที่ยว	(I came here) to travel around.
มาเรียนหนังสือ	(I came here) to study.
มาทำงาน	(I came here) to work.
มาหาเพื่อน	(I came here) to visit a friend/friends.
มาทำธุรกิจ	(I came here) to do business.
คุณพูดภาษาไทยเก่งจัง	You speak Thai so well.
ขอบคุณค่ะ/ครับ ดิฉัน/ผมพูดได้ นิดหน่อย	Thank you. I can speak a little bit.

คุณอยู่เมืองไทยมานานแล้วหรือยัง | Have you been in Thailand for a long time (or not yet)?

นานหลายปีแล้ว | (I've been here) several years already.
ยังไม่นาน | No, not long.
มาอยู่ที่นี่ได้ปีครึ่งแล้ว | I've been here a year and a half already.

GRAMMAR

1. เคย ever

เคย is used to express past experience, namely, that one has done something before, e.g. "I have eaten Thai food." เคย is placed in front of verb. To use เคย, use this pattern.

S (Subject) + เคย + VP (Verb Phrase)

เขาเคยเรียนหนังสือที่กรุงเทพ | He has studied in Bangkok.
ผมเคยมาเที่ยวที่นี่ | I have been here.
ฉันเคยพบเขาแล้ว | I have met him already.
คุณเคยเรียนภาษาไทยไหม | Have you studied Thai (before)?

2. แล้วหรือยัง "already" or "not yet"

แล้วหรือยัง is used to ask questions to learn whether one has done something previously (a) or whether one has done something yet (b).

e.g. "Have you eaten Thai food before?" or "Has he gone yet?"

แล้วหรือยัง is always placed at the end of a sentence. Study examples below.

(a) S + เคย + VP + แล้วหรือยัง

คุณเคยพบเขาแล้วหรือยัง | Have you met him before/previously?
เขาเคยไปเมืองไทยแล้วหรือยัง | Has he been to Thailand before?

To answer the questions above, use these patterns.

Yes:	เคย + (VP) แล้ว
No:	ยังไม่เคย + (VP)

As seen in no. 1, the questions above can also be asked with question word ไหม.

คุณเคยพบเขาไหม | Have you met him previously?
เขาเคยไปเมืองไทยไหม | Has he been to Thailand before?

To answer these questions, use these patterns.

> Yes: เคย + (VP)
>
> No: ไม่เคย + (VP)

(b) S + VP + แล้วหรือยัง

| คุณพบเขาแล้วหรือยัง | Have you met her yet? |
| เขาไปเมืองไทยแล้วหรือยัง | Has she left for Thailand yet? |

To answer these questions, use the following patterns.

> Yes: V+ แล้ว
>
> No: ยัง + ไม่ + V or
>
> ยัง + ไม่ได้ + V

3. กี่ how many

กี่ is used to ask "how many" questions. Classifier is a must when asking a กี่ question.

S + V + DO (direct object) + กี่ + Classifier

คุณมีลูกกี่คน	How many children do you have?
คุณมีปากกากี่ด้าม	How many pens do you have?
คุณเคยมาเมืองไทยกี่ครั้งแล้ว	How many times have you been to Thailand?

To answer, replace กี่ with the answer (number).

ฉันมีลูก ๒ คน	I have two children.
ผมมีปากกา ๕ ด้าม	I have five pens.
ผมเคยมาเมืองไทยหลายครั้ง	I have been to Thailand many times.

4. ก็.....เหมือนกัน also

To say, "I like Thai food also," or "Me too," use ก็.....**เหมือนกัน.**

S + ก็ + VP + เหมือนกัน

เขาก็เคยไปเมืองไทยแล้วเหมือนกัน	She has been to Thailand also.
ฉันก็ชอบอาหารเผ็ดเหมือนกัน	I also like spicy food.
ผมก็แต่งงานแล้วเหมือนกัน	I am also married.

When the topic is already established, the verb phrase can be omitted.

| ผมแต่งงานแล้ว แล้วคุณล่ะ | I'm married. What about you? |
| ผมก็เหมือนกัน | Me too. |

5. ได้, ไม่ได้   can, can't

To say, "I can do something," or " I can't do something," place ได้ or ไม่ได้ at the end of the sentence.

Sentence + ได้
Sentence + ไม่ได้

ฉันพูดไทยได้	I can speak Thai.
เขากินเผ็ดได้	She can eat spicy food.
ฉันพูดภาษาจีนไม่ได้	I cannot speak Chinese.
เขากินเผ็ดไม่ได้	She cannot eat spicy food.

To ask, "Can you do something?" place ได้ไหม at the end of the question.

Sentence + ได้ไหม

คุณพูดไทยได้ไหม	Can you speak Thai?
เขากินเผ็ดได้ไหม	Can he eat spicy food?

Answer Yes: (V) + ได้
No: (V) + ไม่ได้

6. อยาก to want, would like

To say, "I would like to go to Thailand," or "I would like to eat *phad thai*," use อยาก in front of verb.

S + อยาก + VP

e.g. ฉัน (ชั้น) อยากไปเมืองไทย	I would like to go to Thailand.
เขาอยากกินอาหารไทย	She would like to eat Thai food.

Question	อยาก + VP + ไหม	
Answer	Yes:	อยาก (+VP)
	No:	ไม่อยาก (+VP)

e.g. คุณอยากไปเมืองไทยมั้ย	Would you like to go to Thailand?
อยาก (ไป)	Yes.
ไม่อยาก (ไป)	No.

7. Number

Numbers are always placed before a classifier. An exception to this rule is the number one, **หนึ่ง**, which can be placed after a classifier. When that happens, **หนึ่ง** is pronounced as **นึง**.

e.g. เขามีเพื่อนคนไทยหนึ่งคน   She has one Thai friend.

เขามีเพื่อนคนไทยคนนึง   She has a Thai friend.

DRILL

1. เขาเคยไปเมืองไทยแล้วใช่ไหม (yes)

She has been to Thailand, hasn't she?

2. เขาเคยเรียนที่เมืองไทยใช่ไหม (no)

She has studied in Thailand, hasn't she?

3. เขาเคยแต่งงานแล้วใช่ไหม (yes)

She has been married, hasn't she?

4. เขาเคยพบคุณแล้วใช่ไหม (yes)

She has met you already, hasn't she?

5. เขาเคยกินอาหารที่นี่ใช่ไหม (yes)

She has eaten here, hasn't she?

6. เขาเคยอยู่ประเทศฝรั่งเศสใช่ไหม (no)

She has lived in France, hasn't she?

7. เขาเคยพักที่โรงแรมนี้ใช่ไหม (yes)

He has stayed at this hotel, hasn't he?

8. เขาเคยไปเที่ยวประเทศญี่ปุ่นใช่ไหม (yes)

He has been to Japan, hasn't he?

9. เขาเคยทำอาหารไทยใช่ไหม (yes)

He has made Thai food, hasn't he?

10. คุณเคยพบเขาแล้วหรือยัง (yes)

Have you already met him?

11. เขาเคยมีแฟนแล้วหรือยัง (no)

Has he had a girlfriend before?

12. เขาเคยทานอาหารไทยแล้วหรือยัง (yes)

Has he eaten Thai food before?

13. เขาเคยมาเที่ยวที่นี่แล้วหรือยัง (no)

Has he been here before?

PARTNER ACTIVITIES

I. Find out if your partner is single, married, or has a boyfriend/girlfriend.

ขอโทษค่ะ/ครับ   คุณ.....มีแฟนหรือยังคะ/ครับ

แต่งงานแล้วหรือยัง

II. Role Play: Getting To Know Each Other

With a different partner, create a dialogue that includes the following. Then perform it in front of the class.

1. Greeting
2. Name/last name
3. Where they are from
4. Boyfriend/girlfriend/marital status
5. Like/dislike (using และ and/or แต่)
6. Leave taking

Note: You must use question words: ไหม, อะไร, ใช่ไหม, แล้ว.....ล่ะ.

CLASS ACTIVITIES

I. Circulate around the classroom asking questions to find three persons who are married, three who have girlfriends or boyfriends, and three without girlfriends or boyfriends.

	แต่งงานแล้ว	มีแฟนแล้ว	ยังไม่มีแฟน
1.	....	....	....
2.	....	....	....
3.	....	....	....

II. Find the youngest and oldest persons in the classroom.

Oldest person.....

Youngest person.....

GROUP VOCABULARY CHALLENGE

Close your book! Work in groups of four, making a list of questions you are likely to be asked in Thailand. Which group has the most questions? Compare your list with the rest of the class.

NUMBER GAME

Work with your partner. Match the number with the same amount written out in words.

๑๐๙	สิบสองล้านห้าแสนหกหมื่นสี่พันสามร้อยยี่สิบเอ็ด
๑๑,๓๕๐	เก้าสิบห้า
๓๐๔,๗๑๑	เจ็ดพันห้าร้อยห้าสิบห้า
๗,๕๕๕	หนึ่งร้อยเก้า
๑๒,๕๖๔,๓๒๑	สามแสนสี่พันเจ็ดร้อยสิบเอ็ด
	หนึ่งหมื่นหนึ่งพันสามร้อยห้าสิบ

EXERCISES

I. Listening Comprehension

You will hear these sentences in Thai. Number them in the order that you hear them.

.... 1. What is this?

.... 2. What is your name?

.... 3. I do not have a nickname.

.... 4. Hello. How are you?

.... 5. What do you call this in Thai?

.... 6. See you later.

.... 7. How old are you?

.... 8. I do not have a boyfriend/girlfriend.

.... 9. Do you have a nickname?

.... 10. I'm fine. Thank you.

.... 11. What is your last name?

.... 12. What about you?

.... 13. What are you doing here in Thailand?

.... 14. Are you married?

.... 15. I'm going. Bye.

II. Form ten sentences using the words below.

Pronouns:	ฉัน, ผม, ดิฉัน, เขา, เรา, คุณ
Nouns:	คน, เพื่อน, บ้าน, ดินสอ, ปากกา, ประเทศ, เมือง, ชื่อ, ชื่อเล่น, ภาษา, อาหาร, โรงแรม, แฟน
Verbs:	เป็น, ชื่อ, มี, พบ, เจอ, อยาก, ชอบ, มา, พัก, อยู่, พูด, เรียน, ทำ
Stative verbs:	สวย, อร่อย, แพง, ดี, ไทย, อังกฤษ, ฝรั่งเศส, จีน, ญี่ปุ่น, เผ็ด
Adverbs:	เก่ง, มาก, ไม่.....เลย, นิดหน่อย, เคย, ยัง
Prepositions:	จาก, ที่
QW:	อะไร, ไหม, ใช่ไหม, ไหน, เท่าไร, กี่, แล้วหรือยัง
Negatives:	ไม่, ไม่ใช่
Numerals:	หลาย, หนึ่ง, สอง, สาม, สี่, ห้า

1. ....
   ....

2. ....
   ....

3. ....
   ....

4. ....
   ....

5. ....
   ....

6. ....
   ....

7. ....
   ....

8. ....
   ....

9. ....
   ....

10. ....
   ....

CULTURAL CORNER

1. Questions about age are not considered to be rude or nosy. They are some of the ways by which Thai people establish kinship terms. The older person (of the same generation) will be called "พี่" (normally, พี่ + ชื่อ), while the younger one will be called "น้อง" (normally, just the name without the kinship term). The other usual way to establish this relationship is to ask when one graduated from college or school. The one who graduated first will be พี่ and the other will be น้อง. If they are of the same age, Thai people tend to use their names as pronouns instead of ฉัน, คุณ.

2. The Thai number system includes หมื่น for ten thousand, and แสน for a hundred thousand. Be sure to learn these, as they are commonly used.

Unit 2
Family and Relatives

Lesson 5: Family

 คำศัพท์

NOUNS

ครอบครัว (ครอบครัว)	family	ลูกคนเล็ก,ลูกคนสุดท้อง	youngest child
พ่อแม่	parents	ลูกคนที่.....	the.....child
แม่, มารดา	mother	ลูกคนเดียว	the only child
พ่อ, บิดา	father	พี่น้อง	siblings brother/sister
ลูกชาย	son	พี่สาว	older sister
ลูกสาว	daughter	พี่ชาย	older brother
ผู้ชาย	male	น้องสาว	younger sister
ผู้หญิง	female	น้องชาย	younger brother
ลูกคนโต, ลูกคนแรก	first-born child	เด็ก	child
ลูกคนกลาง	middle child	ผู้ใหญ่	adult

*The classifier for human beings is คน.

VERBS

แก่	to be old (used for people)	สนิท	to be intimate, close
อ่อน, เด็ก	to be young	รัก	to love

MISC.

ของ	of
และ, แล้วก็	and (word connector)
มากที่สุด	the most
มากกว่า	V + more than
V + กว่า	V + er
ขวบ	years old (used for children's ages up to twelve. After that, ปี is used.)
เท่านั้น	only
เดียว	one only
ทั้งหมด	altogether

ทั้งสอง	both
หรือ	or

46

QUESTION WORD

หรือเปล่า or not?

QW + **บ้าง** is used when more than one answer is expected.

PATTERNS

คุณมีพี่น้องหรือเปล่า

Do you have siblings?

> มีค่ะ/ครับ ดิฉัน/ผมมีพี่น้อง ๓ คน
>
> Yes, I have three siblings.
>
> (เปล่าค่ะ/ครับ) ดิฉัน/ผมเป็นลูกคนเดียว ไม่มีพี่น้อง
>
> No, I'm an only child. I do not have any siblings.

ครอบครัวของคุณมีทั้งหมดกี่คน

How many people are there in your family altogether?

> ครอบครัวของดิฉัน/ผมมีห้าคน
>
> There are five people in my family.

ครอบครัวคุณมีใครบ้าง

Who is in your family?

> มี พ่อ แม่ พี่สาว ผม/ดิฉัน แล้วก็น้องชาย
>
> There are my dad, mom, my older sister, me, and my younger brother.

คุณมีพี่น้องกี่คน

How many brothers/sisters do you have?

> ดิฉัน/ผมมีพี่สาวคนนึง และน้องชายคนนึง
>
> I have an older sister and a younger brother.
>
> ดิฉัน/ผมมีพี่สาวคนนึง, ดิฉัน/ผมมีพี่สาวคนเดียว
>
> I have an older sister./ I only have an older sister.
>
> ดิฉัน/ผมมีน้องชายคนนึง, ดิฉัน/ผมมีน้องชายคนเดียว
>
> I have a younger brother./ I only have a younger brother.

คุณมีพี่น้องทั้งหมดกี่คน

How many brothers/sisters do you have altogether (counting yourself)?

> มีทั้งหมด ๓ คน
>
> There are three of us.

คุณสนิทกับพ่อแม่ไหม

Are you close to your mom and dad?

    สนิทกับแม่มากกว่าพ่อ

    I'm closer to my mom than my dad.

คุณสนิทกับพ่อหรือแม่

Are you close to your mom or your dad?

    สนิทกับทั้งสอง

    (I'm) close to both (of them).

คุณสนิทกับพี่น้องคนไหนมากที่สุด

Which brothers/sisters are you closest to?

    ดิฉัน/ผม สนิทกับน้องชายคนเล็กมากที่สุด

    I'm closest to my youngest brother.

คุณอ่อนกว่าพี่สาวกี่ปี

How many years younger than your sister are you?

    ดิฉัน/ผมอ่อนกว่าพี่สาว ๓ ปี

    I'm three years younger than my sister.

    ดิฉัน/ผมเด็กกว่าพี่สาวหลายปี

    I'm several years younger than my sister.

คุณแก่กว่าน้องชายกี่ปี

How many years are you older than your brother?

    ดิฉัน/ผมแก่กว่าน้องชาย ๑ ปีเท่านั้น

    I'm only one year older than my younger brother.

พี่น้อง(ของ)คุณแต่งงานแล้วหรือยัง

Are your brothers/sisters married?

    พี่สาวแต่งงานแล้ว แต่น้องชายยังไม่แต่ง

    My older sister is married but my younger brother is not.

คุณแต่งงานมากี่ปีแล้ว

How many years have you been married?

    ดิฉัน/ผมแต่งงานมาได้ ๗ ปีแล้ว

    I've been married for seven years already.

คุณมีลูกกี่คน

How many children do you have?

   มีลูกคนเดียวเท่านั้น

   I have only one child.

ลูกผู้หญิงหรือลูกผู้ชาย

A girl or a boy?

   ลูกผู้ชายค่ะ/ครับ

   A boy.

ลูกคุณอายุกี่ขวบ

How old is your child?

   ห้าขวบค่ะ/ครับ

   Five years old.

ลูกคุณอายุเท่าไรบ้าง

How old are your children?

   คนโตอายุ ๗ ขวบ คนเล็กอายุ ๔ ขวบ

   The first one is seven; the youngest one is four.

GRAMMAR

1. หรือเปล่า or not?

To ask questions like, "Is it good (or not)?" or "Are you American (or not)?" use this pattern.

S + VP + หรือเปล่า
Answer   Yes: (ค่ะ/ครับ) S + VP
No: (เปล่าค่ะ/ครับ) S + ไม่ + VP

e.g. คุณร้อนหรือเปล่า	Are you hot?
(ค่ะ/ครับ) ร้อน	Yes, I'm hot.
(เปล่าค่ะ/ครับ) ดิฉัน/ผมไม่ร้อน	No, I'm not hot.

2. ของ of (possessive marker)

To say, "My mother likes to cook," or "He visited your friends," use ของ in patterns below. ของ can also be omitted as in the first two examples below. When used with question word ใคร, they will form the new question word "whose."

Noun + ของ + Noun or Pronoun

e.g. เพื่อน(ของ)เขาเป็นคนไทย   His friend is Thai.

พี่สาว(ของ)เขาพูดไทยเก่ง   Her older sister can speak Thai well.

นี่ของใคร   Whose is this?

ของฉัน   It's mine.

3. มากกว่า more than

To say, "I worked more than he did," or "I like Thai food more than American food," use this pattern.

S + V (VP) + มากกว่า + Noun or Pronoun

e.g. ฉันกินมากกว่าเขา   I ate more than he did.

เขาเรียนภาษาไทยมากกว่าฉัน   He studies Thai more than I do.

ฉันชอบอาหารไทยมากกว่าอาหารจีน I like Thai food more than Chinese food.

4. มากที่สุด the most

To say, "I worked the most," or "I like Thai food the most," use this pattern.

S + V (VP) + มากที่สุด

e.g. ฉันกินมากที่สุด   I ate the most.

เขาทำงานมากที่สุด   He worked the most.

ฉันชอบภาษาไทยมากที่สุด   I like Thai language the most.

5. กว่า V + er

To make comparisons between two subjects, for example, "I'm older than he is," or "Thai food is spicier than American food," use **กว่า** as in the pattern below.

S + Stative Verb (SV) + กว่า + Noun or Pronoun

e.g. ฉันแก่กว่าเขาห้าปี   I'm five years older than he is.

เมืองไทยร้อนกว่าอเมริกา   Thailand is hotter than America.

ปากกาด้ามนี้แพงกว่าปากกาด้ามนั้น This pen is more expensive than that one.

6. ใคร who?

To ask questions such as, "Who is he?" or "Whom did you stay with?" use the question word **ใคร**. To answer, simply substitute the response for the question word.

e.g. ใครมาเมืองไทย   Who came to Thailand?

     ทอมมาเมืองไทย   Tom came to Thailand.

    เขาคือใคร   Who is he?

      เขาคือพ่อของฉัน   He is my father.

   เขาพักอยู่กับใครที่เมืองไทย   Whom did he stay with in Thailand?

     เขาพักอยู่กับเพื่อนคนไทย   He stayed with (his) Thai friends.

7. Classifier

When nouns are specified in numbers, classifiers are required as in the pattern below.

Noun + Number + Classifier

Question word **กี่** and pre-numeral e.g. **หลาย** (several), **บาง** (some), **ทุก** (every) are considered as numbers, therefore they need to follow the pattern above as well. When noun and classifier are identical, the noun is omitted as in the last example.

e.g. คุณมีพี่น้องกี่คน   How many brothers/sisters do you have?

     ฉันมีพี่สาว ๒ คน   I have two older sisters.

    เขามีเพื่อนคนไทยหลายคน   She has many Thai friends.

    คุณมีปากกากี่ด้าม   How many pens do you have?

    เขาเรียนหลายภาษา   He studies many languages.

8. Ordinal number

To say, "I'm the third child," or "The second son is named Tom," use **ที่** in the pattern below.

Noun + Classifier + ที่ + Number

e.g. ฉันเป็นลูกคนที่สาม   I'm the third child.

    ลูกชายคนที่สองชื่อทอม   The second son is named Tom.

Classifier + แรก can be used instead of clf + ที่ + หนึ่ง

e.g. ลูกคนแรกเป็นผู้หญิง   The eldest child is a girl.

    ลูกคนที่หนึ่งเป็นผู้หญิง   The first child is a girl.

    เขาอยู่บ้านหลังแรก   She lives in the first house.

    เขาอยู่บ้านหลังที่หนึ่ง   She lives in the first house.

9. แล้วก็ and (word connector)

แล้วก็ is similar to และ (and). It is used as a word connector when more than two nouns are mentioned.

e.g. เขาชอบอาหารไทย อาหารเกาหลี แล้วก็ อาหารจีน

He likes Thai, Korean, and Chinese food.

ฉันเคยไปประเทศอังกฤษ เยอรมัน แล้วก็ ฝรั่งเศส

I've been to England, Germany, and France.

10. QW + บ้าง

When บ้าง is placed after a question word, more than one answer is expected.

e.g. คุณเคยไปประเทศไหนบ้าง

Which countries have you been to?

ฉันเคยไปประเทศลาว เวียดนาม แล้วก็กัมพูชา

I've been to Laos, Vietnam, and Cambodia.

คุณมีเพื่อนคนไทยชื่ออะไรบ้าง

What are the names of your Thai friends?

มีชื่อ ตา นิด แอน ต้อง ไก่ แล้วก็ เจ

They are Ta, Nit, Anne, Tong, Kai, and Jey.

DRILL 1

1. ของใคร (mine: ของฉัน)	Whose is this?
2. โรงแรมของใคร (that person)	Whose hotel is it?
3. ปากกาด้ามนี้ของใคร (my friend)	This pen belongs to whom?
4. ลูกของใคร (his)	Whose child?
5. นี่ดินสอของใคร (my mom)	Whose pencil is this?
6. บ้านหลังนี้ของใคร (this person)	This house belongs to whom?

DRILL 2

1. คนนี้สวยไหม	Is this person beautiful?
คนนี้ไม่สวย แต่คนนั้นสวยมาก	No, but that one is very beautiful.
2. ปากกาด้ามนี้แพงไหม	Is that pen expensive?
3. คนนี้เก่งไหม	Is this person skillful?
4. บ้านหลังนี้สวยไหม	Is this house beautiful?
5. คนนี้ดีไหม	Is this person good?
6. โรงแรมนี้แพงไหม	Is this hotel expensive?
7. คนนี้พูดไทยเก่งไหม	Does this person speak Thai well?

DRILL 3

1. แพงหรือเปล่า (yes): แพง | Is it expensive?: Yes, it is.
2. ดีหรือเปล่า (no): ไม่ดี | Is it good?: No, it's not.
3. ร้อนหรือเปล่า (yes) | Are you hot?
4. อร่อยหรือเปล่า (no) | Is it delicious?
5. สนุกหรือเปล่า (yes) | Are you having fun?
6. มีแฟนหรือเปล่า (yes) | Do you have a boyfriend?
7. แฟนสวยหรือเปล่า (yes) | Is your girlfriend pretty?

PARTNER INTERVIEW

Ask your partner the following questions.

1. ครอบครัวคุณมีทั้งหมดกี่คน
2. พ่อแม่คุณอยู่ที่ไหน
3. คุณมีพี่น้องกี่คน มีใครบ้าง
4. คุณสนิทกับใครมากที่สุด

Then compare your family and your partner's family using **และ, มากกว่า, แต่**.

WRITING ASSIGNMENT

Write about you and your family based on the questions above. Then tell the class about your family.

GROUP ACTIVITY

Bring in photos of your family. Show your photos to your group and explain who everyone is.

e.g. คนนี้พ่อ คนนี้แม่ etc.

EXERCISES

I. Listening Comprehension

Ask the teacher questions in order to complete the information below. For example: คนที่หนึ่งชื่ออะไร, คนที่หนึ่งอายุเท่าไร etc.

Name	Age	แฟน's name	No. of children	No. of siblings
คนที่ ๑				
คนที่ ๒				
คนที่ ๓				

53

II. Fill in the blanks.

| กี่ | ไม่........เลย | กว่า | สนิท | แล้วหรือยัง |
| ใคร | มากที่สุด | อายุ | ชอบ | ก็........เหมือนกัน |

1. ขอโทษ คุณ.............เท่าไร: ดิฉันอายุ ๒๕ ปีค่ะ
2. คุณมีปากกา.............ด้าม: มีปากกา ๒ ด้าม
3. คุณ.............อาหารจีนไหม: ชอบมากครับ
4. เขา.............ชอบอาหารไทย.............
5. เขาเคยไปเมืองไทย.............: ยังค่ะ   เขายังไม่เคยไปเมืองไทย
6. คุณมีพี่น้องหรือเปล่า: เปล่าครับ   ผม.............มีพี่น้อง.............
7. คุณสนิทกับพ่อแม่ไหม: ....ครับ
8. บ้านหลังนี้ของ.............: ของคุณจอห์น
9. ฉันชอบอาหารไทย.............
10. อาหารไทยเผ็ด.............อาหารอเมริกา

III. The dialogue below is out of order. Please reorder it correctly.

.............: ค่ะ แล้วคุณล่ะ
.............: ขอโทษค่ะ คุณอายุเท่าไรคะ
.............: ดิฉันเป็นลูกคนเดียวค่ะ
.............: คุณเป็นลูกคนสุดท้องหรือคะ
.............: ๒๕ ปีค่ะ แล้วคุณล่ะ
.............: มีพี่สาวสองคนค่ะ
.............: ดิฉันอายุ ๓๐ ปีค่ะ
.............: คุณมีพี่น้องกี่คนคะ

EXTRA VOCABULARY

พ่อเลี้ยง	stepfather
แม่เลี้ยง	stepmother
ลูกเลี้ยง	stepchild
ลูก/บุตรบุญธรรม	adopted child
พี่น้องต่างพ่อ	siblings with different father
พี่น้องต่างแม่	siblings with different mother
เลิก/หย่า	to divorce

Lesson 6: Relatives

 คำศัพท์

NOUNS

(คุณ)ปู่	paternal grandfather
(คุณ)ย่า	paternal grandmother
(คุณ)ตา	maternal grandfather
(คุณ)ยาย	maternal grandmother
ปู่ย่าตายาย	grandparents
ป้า	elder sister of mother or father
ลุง	elder brother of mother or father
น้า (น้าสาว น้าชาย)	younger sister or brother of mother
อา (อาผู้หญิง อาผู้ชาย)	younger sister or brother of father
หลานสาว	niece, granddaughter
หลานชาย	nephew, grandson
ลูกพี่ลูกน้อง	cousins
ญาติ	relatives
ญาติข้างพ่อ	relatives on father's side
ญาติข้างแม่	relatives on mother's side
สามี	husband
ภริยา, ภรรยา	wife
สะใภ้	female in-law
เขย	male in-law

*The classifier for human beings is คน.

VERB

เสีย   to pass away, to be out of order (e.g. TV, radio), to be spoiled (e.g. food)

56

MISC.

ยัง	still
ทั้ง.....และ	both.....and

PATTERNS

พ่อของพ่อเรียกว่าอะไร   What do you call the father of one's father?

   พ่อของพ่อเรียกว่า ปู่

แม่ของแม่เรียกว่าอะไร   What do you call the mother of one's mother?

   แม่ของแม่เรียกว่า ยาย

สามีของพี่สาวเรียกว่า พี่เขย
สามีของป้าเรียกว่า ลุงเขย
สามีของน้าเรียกว่า น้าเขย
สามีของอาเรียกว่า อาเขย
ภริยาของน้องชายเรียกว่า น้องสะใภ้
ภริยาของลุงเรียกว่า ป้าสะใภ้
ภริยาของน้าเรียกว่า น้าสะใภ้
ภริยาของอาเรียกว่า อาสะใภ้

ปู่ย่าตายาย (ของ) คุณยังอยู่ไหม

Are your grandparents still alive?

   คุณตา คุณยาย ยังอยู่ แต่ คุณปู่คุณย่าเสียแล้ว

   My maternal grandparents are still alive but my paternal grandparents have already passed away.

คุณสนิทกับตาหรือยาย

Are you close to your maternal grandfather or grandmother?

   สนิทกับทั้งตาและยาย

   I'm close to both my maternal grandfather and grandmother.

   สนิทกับทั้งสอง (คน)

   I'm close to both of them.

ตากับยายคุณอยู่ที่ไหน

Where do your maternal grandfather and grandmother live?

ตากับยายอยู่กับเราที่บ้าน

They live with us at home.

GRAMMAR

1. ทั้ง.....และ both.....and

To say, "I like both Thai food and Chinese food," or "Both my mom and dad work here," use **ทั้ง.....และ** in patterns below.

> S + V + ทั้ง + Object 1 + และ + Object 1
> ทั้ง + Subject 1 + และ + Subject 2 + VP

ฉันชอบทั้งอาหารไทยและอาหารจีน   I like both Thai (food) and Chinese food.
ทั้งพ่อและแม่ทำงานที่นี่   Both my mom and dad work here.

When the subject is established, one can use **ทั้งสอง** instead of **ทั้ง.....และ**

คุณชอบอาหารไทยหรืออาหารจีน   Do you like Thai (food) or Chinese food?
    ฉันชอบทั้งสอง   I like them both.
พ่อแม่คุณทำงานที่ไหน   Where do your parents work?
    ทั้งสองทำงานที่นี่   Both work here.

2. หรือ or

To ask questions like, "Do you like Thai food or Chinese food?" or "Do you live here or in Thailand?" **หรือ** can be used as in the pattern below.

> S + V + Object 1 + หรือ + Object 2
> S1 + หรือ + S2 + VP

To answer, state subject or object of your choice.

คุณชอบอาหารไทยหรืออาหารจีน   Do you like Thai (food) or Chinese food?
    อาหารไทย   (I like) Thai food.
    ชอบทั้งอาหารจีนและอาหารไทย   (I) like both Chinese and Thai.
    ไม่ชอบทั้งสอง ฉันชอบอาหารอเมริกัน   I don't like either. I like American food.

พ่อหรือแม่ทำงานที่นี่	Who works here, your mother or father?
แม่	My mom (works) here.
ทั้งพ่อและแม่ทำงานที่นี่	Both my mom and dad work here.
ทั้งสองไม่ได้ทำงานที่นี่	Neither works here.

DRILL 1

1. พ่อของพ่อเรียกว่าอะไร
   พ่อของพ่อเรียกว่า ปู่
2. แม่ของพ่อเรียกว่าอะไร (ย่า)
3. พ่อของแม่เรียกว่าอะไร (ตา)
4. แม่ของแม่เรียกว่าอะไร (ยาย)
5. พี่สาวของพ่อเรียกว่าอะไร (ป้า)
6. พี่ชายของพ่อเรียกว่าอะไร (ลุง)
7. น้องชายน้องสาวของพ่อเรียกว่าอะไร (อา)
8. พี่สาวของแม่เรียกว่าอะไร (ป้า)
9. พี่ชายของแม่เรียกว่าอะไร (ลุง)
10. น้องชายและน้องสาวของแม่เรียกว่าอะไร (น้า)

DRILL 2

1. เขามีเพื่อน: เขามีเพื่อนกี่คน She has friends: How many friends does she have?
2. คนนี้มีลูก This person has children.
3. เขามีบ้าน He has a house.
4. คุณมีแฟน You have boyfriends/girlfriends.
5. คนนั้นมีปากกา That person has a pen.

DRILL 3

1. เขาแต่งงานแล้วใช่ไหม (no)
   He is (already) married, isn't he?
       ไม่ใช่ เขายังไม่ได้แต่งงาน
       No, he is not (yet) married.
2. เขาไปเมืองไทยแล้วใช่ไหม (no)
   He went to Thailand (already), didn't he?
3. เพื่อนคุณไปอังกฤษแล้วใช่ไหม (no)
   Your friend (already) went to England, didn't she?

4. คนนี้ชื่อทอมใช่ไหม (no)

   This person's name is Tom, isn't it?

5. คนนี้เป็นแฟนคุณใช่ไหม (no)

   This person is your girlfriend, isn't she?

6. คุณสนิทกับพี่เขยใช่ไหม (no)

   You are close to your brother-in-law, aren't you?

7. เขามาจากอเมริกาใช่ไหม (no)

   She came from America, didn't she?

8. เพื่อนคุณเคยมาเมืองไทยแล้วใช่ไหม (yes)

   Your friend has been to Thailand, hasn't he?

9. คุณชอบเรียนภาษาไทยใช่ไหม (yes)

   You like to study Thai, don't you?

10. คุณอยากไปเมืองไทยใช่ไหม (yes)

    You would like to go to Thailand, wouldn't you?

11. พี่สะใภ้คุณอยู่ประเทศอังกฤษใช่ไหม (yes)

    Your sister-in-law lives in England, doesn't she?

12. ปู่ย่าตายายคุณยังอยู่ใช่ไหม (yes)

    Your grandparents are still alive, aren't they?

PARTNER ACTIVITIES

I. Work with your partner. Fill in the blanks below.

อาเป็น ....

ปู่เป็น ....

ตาเป็น ....

ป้าเป็น ....

ลุงเป็น ....

ย่าเป็น ....

ยายเป็น ....

II. Look at this family tree, then write down appropriate kinship terms for **มานะ**.

มานะ

III. Work with your partner. Fill in the family tree with the information below.

มานะเป็นลูกคนกลางอายุ ๑๐ ปี เขามีพี่สาวหนึ่งคน และน้องสาวหนึ่งคน พี่สาวแก่กว่า
มานะ ๑ ปี ชื่อมาลัย น้องสาวอ่อนกว่ามานะ ๕ ปี ชื่อมาลี

พ่อมานะชื่อสิน สินอายุ ๓๕ ปี เขามีพี่สาวหนึ่งคน และน้องสาวหนึ่งคน พี่สาวสินชื่อออน
อายุ ๓๗ ปี น้องสาวชื่อใหม่ อายุ ๓๐ ปี พ่อแม่ของสินชื่อทา และวัน ทาแก่กว่าวัน ๕ ปี วัน
อายุ ๗๐ ปี

แม่ของมานะชื่อดาว ดาวเป็นลูกคนที่ ๓ พ่อดาวชื่อเอก อายุ ๗๒ ปี แม่ดาวชื่อ มา
มาอายุอ่อนกว่าสามี ๓ ปี

เอกและมา มีลูก ๔ คน ลูกคนโตเป็นผู้ชายชื่อดอน อายุ ๓๔ ปี เดือนเป็นลูกคนที่สอง
อายุอ่อนกว่าดอน ๒ ปี แดงเป็นลูกคนสุดท้อง อายุ ๒๒ ปี อ่อนกว่าดาว ๖ ปี

IV. Teacher, using kinship terms, asks students questions based on the information
above.

e.g. ปู่ของมานะชื่ออะไร, ปู่ของมานะอายุเท่าไหร่ etc.

KINSHIP TERM BINGO

Each student randomly fills in the grid below with the kinship terms provided. Some kinship terms may be used more than once, in order to complete the grid. The teacher calls out kinship term definitions, one by one, and students cross out the term on their grids corresponding to the definition. For example, if the teacher says น้องของแม่, students will cross out น้า. This game can be played until several students get "bingo."

BINGO GRID

		FREE		

KINSHIP TERMS

ปู่	ยาย	ย่า	ตา	ลุง	ป้า
น้า	อา	พี่เขย	พี่สะใภ้	ลูกพี่ลูกน้อง	
หลานชาย	หลานสาว				

CLASS ACTIVITY

Circulate around the classroom to find two persons who.....

1. .... are an only child.
2. .... have grandparents who are still alive.
3. .... have parents who live in Seattle.
4. .... are the oldest child.
5. .... are the youngest child.
6. .... are married.

CULTURAL CORNER

Kinship terms are very important in Thai since they are often used as pronouns instead of the common "you" and "I." For example, Thais will never call their mother or father "you" and will never refer to themselves as "I" when talking to parents. Instead, they will use "แม่" or "พ่อ" in place of second-person pronouns, and use their names or "ลูก" in place of first-person pronouns.

e.g. แม่หิวหรือยังคะ   Are you hungry (Mom)?
      ลูกหิวแล้ว   I'm hungry already.

The use of kinship terms is not only limited to members of the family. For example, Thais will call an older acquaintance "พี่." Therefore, when a Thai meets someone, he/she needs to determine that person's age in order to use the proper kinship term to show intimacy. Someone who appears to be older than one's parents will be called "ป้า" or "ลุง." Someone younger than one's parents will be called "น้า." Interestingly, maternal kinship terms are normally used as pronouns, not paternal ones. When age is not clear, Thais will ask how old one is or what year one graduated from high school or college. Thais tend to refer to their friend's family members the same way their friend does. So when you are with Thai friends, just follow their lead!

Lesson 7: What Do They Look Like?

((●)) คำศัพท์

VERBS

(ไว้) ผม	(to have) ..... hair
สั้น	to be short
ยาว	to be long
ไว้หนวด	to have a mustache
ไว้เครา	to have a beard
สวย	to be beautiful
หล่อ	to be handsome
หน้าตาดี	to be good looking
น่ารัก	to be cute
สูง	to be tall
เตี้ย	to be short
ไม่สูงไม่เตี้ย	to be average in height (not tall, not short)
อ้วน	to be chubby, fat
ผอม	to be thin
ไม่อ้วนไม่ผอม	to be average in weight (not fat, not thin)
ท้วม	to be plump
ล่ำ	to be muscular
ตัวใหญ่	to have a big body, frame (ใหญ่, to be big)
ตัวเล็ก	to have a small body, frame (เล็ก, to be small)
รูปร่างหน้าตา	physical appearance

QUESTION WORDS

ใคร/อะไร.....กว่ากัน/ที่สุด	comparison question
แค่ไหน	how.....?

PRONOUN

พวกเขา/พวกเค้า	they

64

MISC.

ที่สุด	-est
เท่ากับ/เท่ากัน	to be equal in..... (e.g. height, weight)
เหมือนกับ/เหมือนกัน	to be the same
คล้ายกับ/คล้ายกัน	to be similar
ต่างกับ/ต่างกัน	to be different
ตรงไหน	(exactly) where
ไม่.....ไม่.....	neither.....nor.....

PATTERNS

เขารูปร่างหน้าตาเป็นยังไงคะ/ครับ	What does he look like?
เขาไว้ผมสั้น	He has short hair.
เขาไม่มีหนวดไม่มีเครา	He does not have a mustache and beard.
เขาไม่ไว้หนวดแต่ไว้เครา	He doesn't have a mustache, but he has a beard.
เอกับบี ใครสูงกว่ากัน	Who is taller, A or B?
เอสูงกว่าบีนิดหน่อย	A is a little taller than B.
เอกับบีสูงเท่ากัน	A and B are of the same height.
เอสูงเท่ากับบี	A is as tall as B.
พี่สาวคุณเหมือนกันตรงไหน	How (in what way) are your sisters exactly the same?
ทั้งสองไว้ผมยาวเหมือนกัน	Both have long hair.
พวกเขาผมยาวเหมือนกัน	They both have long hair.
พี่สาวคุณต่างกันตรงไหน	How (in what way) are your sisters different?
พี่คนที่หนึ่งสูง แต่คนที่สองเตี้ย	The first sister is tall but the second one is short.
ผม/ดิฉันคล้ายกับพ่อมากกว่าแม่	I'm more similar (in appearance) to my dad than my mom.
ผม/ดิฉันกับพ่อคล้ายกัน	I'm similar (in appearance) to my dad.
พี่น้องคุณ ใครสูงที่สุด	Who is tallest among your siblings?
น้องชายสูงที่สุด	My younger brother is the tallest.
คนไหนสูงกว่ากัน พี่สาวหรือน้องสาว	Which one is taller, your older or younger sister?
พี่สาวสูงกว่า	My older sister is taller.

65

ใครสูงที่สุด พี่สาว คุณ หรือ น้องสาว	Who is the tallest, your older sister, you, or your younger sister?
พี่สาวสูงที่สุด	My older sister is the tallest.
ใครพูดไทยเก่งกว่ากัน คุณ หรือน้องสาว	Who speaks better Thai, you or your sister?
ดิฉัน/ผมพูดไทยเก่งกว่าน้อง	I speak Thai better than my sister.
เขาสูงแค่ไหน	How tall is he?
เขาสูง ๑๙๐ เซนติเมตร	He is 190 centimeters tall.
เขาสูงแค่นี้	He is this tall.

GRAMMAR

1. กว่ากัน Comparison questions

To ask comparison questions such as, "Who is taller?", "Who is bigger?", or "Which one is better?", use **กว่ากัน** with question words **ใคร**, **อะไร**, or **Clf. + ไหน** as in these patterns.

$$S1 + กับ + S2$$
$$QW + SV \text{ (Stative Verb)} + กว่ากัน$$
or
$$QW + SV + กว่ากัน$$
$$S1 + หรือ + S2$$
Answer $\quad S1 + SV + กว่า + S2$
or
$$S2 + SV + กว่า + S1$$

e.g. คนนี้กับคนนั้น ใครสวยกว่ากัน

Who is prettier, this person or that person?

คนนี้สวยกว่า (คนนั้น)

This person is prettier (than that person).

คนไหนสูงกว่ากัน พี่สาวหรือน้องสาว

Who is taller, your older sister or younger sister?

พี่สาวสูงกว่า (น้องสาว)

My older sister is taller.

อาหารไทยกับอาหารจีน อะไรเผ็ดกว่ากัน

Which is spicier, Thai (food) or Chinese food?

อาหารไทยเผ็ดกว่า

Thai food is spicier.

2. ที่สุด -est

To ask superlative questions such as, "Who is tallest?" or "Which pen is the most expensive?" use **ที่สุด** with question word **ใคร**, **อะไร**, or **Clf. + ไหน** as in these patterns.

S1, S2, และ S3

QW + SV + ที่สุด

or

QW + SV + ที่สุด

S1, S2, หรือ S3

Answer S + SV + ที่สุด

---

e.g. คุณทอม คุณโจ และ คุณจอห์น ใครสูงที่สุด

Who is the tallest, Tom, Joe, or John?

คุณทอมสูงที่สุด

Tom is the tallest.

คนไหนสูงที่สุด คุณ น้องสาว หรือ พี่ชาย

Which one is tallest, you, your sister, or your brother?

ฉันสูงที่สุด

I'm the tallest.

3. เท่ากับ/เท่ากัน, เหมือนกับ/เหมือนกัน, คล้ายกับ/คล้ายกัน to be equal, to be the same, to be similar

เท่ากับ and **เท่ากัน** means to be equal or to be the same in size or quantity that can be measured in numbers e.g. height, weight, prices, etc.

เท่ากับ/เท่ากัน are more specific than **เหมือนกับ/เหมือนกัน**. For example, "เขาทั้งสองสูงเท่ากัน" means "Both of them are of the same height." "เขาทั้งสองสูงเหมือนกัน" does not necessarily mean that they are of the same height. It means that "They are both tall."

Use the patterns below when using เท่ากับ/เท่ากัน or เหมือนกับ/เหมือนกัน.

S1 กับ S2 + V + เท่ากัน

S1 กับ S2 + V + เหมือนกัน

S1 + V + เท่ากับ + S2

S1 + V + เหมือนกับ + S2

---

e.g. คนนี้กับคนนั้นสูง**เท่ากัน**

This person and that person are of the same height.

คนนี้สูง**เท่ากับ**คนนั้น

This person is as tall as that one.

คนนี้กับคนนั้นสูง**เหมือนกัน**

คนนี้สูง**เหมือนกับ**คนนั้น

This person and that person are tall. (Both of them are tall but might not be the same height).

ปากกาด้ามนี้กับปากกาด้ามนั้นแพง**เท่ากัน**

This pen and that pen are as expensive (are the same price).

ปากกาด้ามนี้แพง**เท่ากับ**ปากกาด้ามนั้น

This pen is as expensive as that one.

ปากกาด้ามนี้กับปากกาด้ามนั้นแพง**เหมือนกัน**

ปากกาด้ามนี้แพง**เหมือนกับ**ปากกาด้ามนั้น

This pen and that pen are expensive. (Both are expensive but might not cost exactly the same).

DRILL

1. แม่กับลูกใครสูงกว่ากัน (ลูก)
   Who is taller, mother or daughter?

2. ลูกกับพ่อ ใครเตี้ยกว่ากัน (พ่อ)
   Who is shorter, the son or the father?

3. พี่ชายกับน้องชาย ใครตัวใหญ่กว่ากัน (พี่ชาย)
   Who is bigger, the older brother or younger brother?

4. พี่สาวกับน้องสาว ใครผมยาวกว่ากัน (น้องสาว)
   Who has longer hair, the older sister or younger sister?

5. พี่สาวกับน้องสาว ใครสวยกว่ากัน (เท่ากัน)
   Who is prettier, the older sister or younger sister?

6. พี่ชายกับน้องชาย ใครสูงกว่ากัน (เท่ากับ)
   Who is taller, the older brother or younger brother?

7. พ่อกับแม่ คุณสนิทกับใครมากกว่ากัน (แม่)
   To whom are you closer, your mom or your dad?

8. แล้วตากับยายล่ะ (ตา)
   What about grandfather and grandmother?

9. คนไหนอ้วนกว่ากัน พี่ชายหรือน้องชาย (พี่ชาย)

Who is fatter, the older brother or younger brother?

10. แล้วใครสูงกว่ากัน (น้องชาย)

And who is taller?

PARTNER ACTIVITIES

I. Practice with your partner, using คนที่ ๑, คนที่ ๒ etc. to describe the physical appearance of the people below.

II. Practice comparing these people, using vocabulary and sentence structures above (ใคร..... กว่ากัน, ใคร..... ที่สุด, คนที่..... V + กว่า คนที่..... etc.)

III. Describe the physical appearance of your family members to your partner.

EXERCISES

I. Listening Comprehension

You will hear these sentences in Thai. Number the sentences in the order that you hear them.

.... 1. How many brothers and sisters do you have?

.... 2. What are you doing in Thailand?

.... 3. Have you been to Thailand?

69

.... 4. My older brother is taller than I am.

.... 5. How old are you?

.... 6. I've been to Thailand several times.

.... 7. I like Thai food the most.

.... 8. My sister is prettier than I am.

.... 9. Where do your parents live?

.... 10. I'm closer to my dad than my mom.

.... 11. I have lots of Thai friends.

.... 12. I also like spicy food.

.... 13. Who is taller, you or your younger sister?

.... 14. We are of the same height.

II. Make up sentences with the words below.

1.   ไหน (which)

2.   นั้น

3.   ไม่ได้

4.   มากที่สุด

5.   กว่า

6.   กว่ากัน

7.   เคย

8.   แล้วหรือยัง

9.   เท่ากับ

10. เท่ากัน

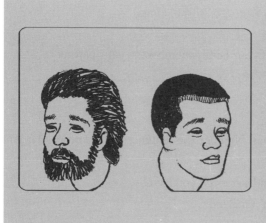

CULTURAL CORNER

   Thai people are not as sensitive about physical characteristics as Americans are. Thais will sometimes comment humorously about someone's big nose, their height and weight, etc. This can make visitors uncomfortable but it is meant in good fun!!

Lesson 8: What Are They Like?

((●)) คำศัพท์

VERBS

ดี	to be good
ดุ	to be strict
ใจดี	to be kind, generous
ใจกว้าง	to be generous, open-minded
ใจแคบ	to be narrow-minded
ใจเย็น	to be patient
ใจร้อน	to be hot tempered
ขยัน	to be diligent
ขี้เกียจ	to be lazy
ขี้อาย	to be shy all the time/easily
ช่างพูด/ช่างคุย	to be chatty, talkative
น่ารัก	to be lovable, cute
ร่าเริง	to be cheerful
ขี้บ่น	to be given to complaining
ขี้โมโห	to be angry easily
ขี้เหนียว	to be stingy
ขี้เกรงใจ	to be considerate
ขี้หงุดหงิด	to be moody, agitated easily
ขี้เล่น	to be playful
ดื้อ	to be stubborn

PRONOUNS

ท่าน   you, she/he

MISC.

ไม่ใช่หรือ negative tag question

PATTERNS

อาจารย์ (ของ) คุณเป็นคนยังไงคะ/ครับ

แม่   "

พ่อ   "

What type of person is your teacher/mother/father?

ท่านใจดี   He/she is kind.

  ดุ   He/she is strict.

  ใจเย็น   He/she is patient.

เขาเป็นคนยังไง   What type of person is she?

  เขาเป็นคนดี   She is a good person.

  เขาเป็นคนดุ   She is a strict person.

  เขาเป็นคนใจเย็น   She is a patient person.

  เขาเป็นคนใจร้อน   She is a hot-tempered person.

  เขาทั้งใจดีและใจเย็น   She is both kind and patient.

พ่อคุณใจดีไม่ใช่หรือ   Your father is kind, isn't he?

  ใช่ค่ะ/ครับ ท่านใจดีมาก   Yes, he is very kind.

พี่สาวคุณขี้อายไม่ใช่หรือ   Your older sister is shy, isn't she?

  ใช่ เขาขี้อายมาก   Yes, she is very shy.

  ไม่ใช่ เขาไม่ขี้อายเลย   No, she is not shy at all.

พ่อกับแม่คุณ ใครใจดีกว่ากัน   Who is kinder (less strict), your dad or your mom?

  แม่ใจดีกว่าพ่อ   My mom is kinder (less strict).

ใครช่างพูดกว่ากัน คุณหรือน้องสาว Who is more talkative, you or your sister?

  น้องสาวช่างพูดมากกว่า   My younger sister is more talkative.

พี่คุณเป็นคนยังไง   What type of persons are your older siblings?

  พวกเขาขี้อายเหมือนกัน   They are all shy.

GRAMMAR

1. เป็น   to be (something or someone)

To say, "He is a good person," or "She is my sister," use the pattern.

S + เป็น + Noun Complement

e.g. เขาเป็นคนดี   He is a good person.

คนนี้เป็นพี่สาวของฉัน   This person is my (older) sister.

เขาเป็นคนไทย   He is Thai.

Note: To say, "He is good," or "He is kind," เป็น is not needed.

2. ไม่ใช่หรือ

To ask a question like, "He is your brother, isn't he?" or "She likes Thai food, doesn't she?" use ไม่ใช่หรือ as question tag.

S + V + DO + ไม่ใช่หรือ

S + VP + ไม่ใช่หรือ

Answer   Yes: ใช่ S + V + DO or S + VP

No: ไม่ใช่ S + ไม่ or ไม่ได้ + V + DO

or S + ไม่ or ไม่ได้ + VP

เขาเป็นคนไทยไม่ใช่หรือ(รึ)

He is Thai, isn't that right?

ไม่ใช่ เขาไม่ใช่คนไทย / เขาไม่ได้เป็นคนไทย

No, he is not Thai.

คนนี้เรียนภาษาจีนไม่ใช่หรือ(รึ)

This person studies Chinese, isn't that right?

ใช่ เขาเรียนภาษาจีน

Yes, he studies Chinese.

ไม่ใช่ เขาไม่ได้เรียนภาษาจีน เขาเรียนภาษาไทย

No, he doesn't study Chinese. He studies Thai.

ไม่ใช่ เขาเรียนภาษาไทย ไม่ใช่ภาษาจีน

No, he studies Thai, not Chinese.

DRILL 1

1. เขาเป็นใคร (พ่อ): เขาเป็นพ่อของฉัน

2. พ่อไปไหน (เมืองจีน) Where did your dad go? (China)

3. ใครไปเมืองจีน (พ่อ) Who went to China? (dad)

4. พ่อไปเมืองจีนกับใคร (กับแม่) With whom did your dad go to China? (mom)

5. พ่อไปเมืองจีนกับแม่ใช่ไหม (ใช่) Your dad went to China with your mom, right? (yes)

6. พ่อไปทำอะไรที่เมืองจีน (ธุรกิจ) What did your dad (go to) do in China? (business)

7. ใครทำธุรกิจที่เมืองจีน (พ่อ) Who did business in China? (dad)

8. พ่อทำธุรกิจที่ประเทศอะไร (จีน) In what country did your dad do business? (China)

DRILL 2

1. เขาชอบเมืองไทยหรือ (yes): เขาชอบเมืองไทย

2. เขาน่ารักหรือ (no) Is she cute?

3. แฟนเขาสวยหรือ (yes) Is his girlfriend pretty?

4. อาหารแพงหรือ (no) Is the food expensive?

5. เมืองไทยสนุกหรือ (yes) Is Thailand fun?

6. อาหารอร่อยหรือ (yes) Is the food delicious?

7. เขาพักที่โรงแรมหรือ (no) Is he staying at a hotel?

DRILL 3

1. เขาไปเมืองไทยกับเพื่อนไม่ใช่หรือ (yes)

   He went to Thailand with his friends, didn't he?

2. พ่อกับเขาสนิทกันมากไม่ใช่หรือ (yes)

   He and his dad are very close, aren't they?

3. แฟนคุณชอบอาหารไทยไม่ใช่หรือ (no, she likes Chinese food)

   Your แฟน likes Thai food, doesn't she?

4. คุณมีแฟนแล้วไม่ใช่หรือ (no, I don't have one yet)

   You already have a boyfriend/girlfriend, don't you?

5. เขาทำธุรกิจที่เมืองไทยไม่ใช่หรือ (no, she studies in Thailand)

   She does business in Thailand, doesn't she?

6. เขาพูดภาษาไทยเก่งไม่ใช่หรือ (no, she speaks Korean well)

   She speaks Thai well, doesn't she?

PARTNER ACTIVITY

Ask your partner about his/her parents (พ่อแม่ของคุณเป็นคนยังไง). Compare them with yours. Report to the class, using the pattern below.

e.g. ทั้ง แม่ของผม และ แม่ของคุณใจดี

แม่ของผมใจดี แต่ แม่ของคุณดุ

ทั้ง................................และ..............................

.............................แต่..............................

GOSSIP GAME

Teacher makes up a message. Students divide up into groups of six or seven. Teacher whispers the message to the leader of each group, each of whom passes it on to a team mate, who in turn passes the message on, one by one. Whose final message is the most correct?

EXERCISES

I. Reading Comprehension

Read the following passage. Then answer the questions in English.

พ่อของฉันดุแต่เป็นคนดีและคุยสนุกมาก   แม่ของฉันน่ารัก   ใจดีและชอบทำอาหาร   แม่ทำอาหารไทยเก่งมาก

ฉันเป็นลูกคนกลางอายุ ๑๘ ปี เป็นคนช่างพูดช่างคุย พี่สาวแก่กว่าฉัน ๔ ปี เขาเป็นคนร่าเริงแต่ใจร้อน น้องชายของฉันอ่อนกว่าฉัน ๓ ปี เป็นคนขี้อายไม่ช่างพูด แต่เรียนเก่งมาก ฉันสนิทกับพ่อแม่มากแต่ไม่สนิทกับน้องชาย

1. How many are there in this family?
2. How old is the person who wrote the story? Is he/she the youngest or the oldest child?
3. Describe his/her father.
4. Describe his/her mother.
5. How old is his/her sister? What type of person is she?
6. How old is his/her brother? What type of person is he?
7. Is the writer close to everyone in the family?

II. Listening Comprehension

Using kinship terms, ask your teacher questions to find out names, ages, and personal characteristics of these people in your family tree.

e.g. ตาชื่ออะไร, ท่านอายุเท่าไร, ท่านเป็นคนยังไง

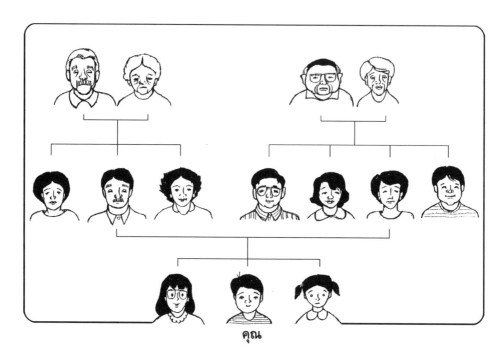

คุณ

III. Writing Exercise

Write about your close friend (เพื่อนสนิท), including name, age, personality, and appearance.

เพื่อนสนิทของฉันชื่อ...

....

....

....

....

....

CULTURAL CORNER

1. Like "แม่" and "พ่อ", the kinship terms (ปู่, ย่า, ตา, ยาย) can be used as second-person pronouns.

ท่าน is used as a third-person pronoun when one refers to one's grandparents.

2. Thais tend to value modesty (ความถ่อมตน). They will not openly give compliments to themselves or to their family members (e.g. I can speak English well or my daughter is very beautiful) even if they are true because it will be considered bragging (ขี้โม้, ขี้คุย). When given compliments, Thais tend to be reluctant to accept them.

Lesson 9: Occupations

((•)) คำศัพท์

NOUNS

อาชีพ (อาชีพ)	occupation
อาจารย์	college professor
ครู	school teacher
นักศึกษา	university student
นักเรียน	student
นักบิน	pilot
นักร้อง	singer
ข้าราชการ	government official
นักธุรกิจ	businessman
หมอ, แพทย์	physician, doctor
หมอฟัน	dentist
พยาบาล	nurse
วิศวกร	engineer
สถาปนิก	architect
ทนายความ	attorney
ทหาร	soldier
ตำรวจ	policeman
เลขา[นุการ]	secretary
แม่บ้าน	housewife
ผู้จัดการ	manager
พนักงาน/เจ้าหน้าที่	an official, person in charge
พ่อค้า/แม่ค้า	male/female vendor
พ่อครัว/แม่ครัว	male/female chef, cook
ช่างไม้	carpenter
ช่างไฟฟ้า	electrician
ช่างเครื่อง	mechanic

ช่างประปา	plumber
ช่างถ่ายรูป	photographer
บุรุษไปรษณีย์	postman

*The classifier for human beings is คน.

บริษัท (บริษัท, แห่ง)	company
โรงพยาบาล (โรงพยาบาล, แห่ง)	hospital
คลินิก (แห่ง,คลินิก)	clinic
ร้านอาหาร (ร้าน)	restaurant
ธนาคาร (ธนาคาร, แห่ง)	bank
มหาวิทยาลัย (มหาวิทยาลัย, แห่ง)	university
โรงเรียน (โรงเรียน, โรง, แห่ง)	school
วิชา (วิชา)	subject

*Words in parentheses are classifiers.

VERBS

แข็งแรง	to be strong	อดทน	to endure
ฉลาด	to be smart	เกษียณ	to retire
สอน	to teach		

PRE-VERBS

ต้อง	must	เพิ่ง	just

QUESTION WORDS

มานานเท่าไรแล้ว	for how long (has one done something)?
มานานกี่ปีแล้ว	for how many years (has one done something)?

MISC.

ที่	which, who, that
เดียวกัน	the same

PREFIX

นัก..........,	ช่าง......

((•))) PATTERNS

เขาทำงานอะไร   What does she do?

เขามีอาชีพอะไร   What is her occupation?
   เขาเป็นหมอ   She is a doctor.
   เขาเป็นนักธุรกิจ   She is a businessman/woman.
   เขาเป็นผู้จัดการธนาคาร   She is a bank manager.
   เขาเป็นพนักงานโรงแรม   She is a hotel clerk.
   เขาทำร้านอาหาร   She runs a restaurant.
   เขาทำ(บริษัท)ทัวร์   She runs a tour company.
   เขาทำธุรกิจ   She runs a business.

เขาทำงานที่นี่มานานเท่าไหร่แล้ว

How long has he worked here?
   เขาทำงานที่นี่มาได้ ๕ ปีแล้ว
     He has worked here five years.

เขาทำงานที่นี่มานานแล้วหรือยัง

Has he worked here long?
   เขาเพิ่งทำ
     He just started.

เขาเป็นอาจารย์ที่ไหน

Where is she a professor?
   เขาเป็นอาจารย์ที่มหาวิทยาลัยวอชิงตัน
     She is a professor at University of Washington.
เขาสอนวิชาอะไร

What does she teach?
   เขาสอนวิชาภาษาไทย
     She teaches Thai.
เขาสอนภาษาไทยมากี่ปีแล้ว
     How many years has she taught Thai?
   เขาสอนภาษาไทยมาสิบปีแล้ว
     She has taught Thai for ten years.

คนที่เป็นหมอต้องเป็นคนยังไง

What type of person must a doctor be?

    คนที่เป็นหมอต้องฉลาด

    A person who is a doctor must be smart.

คนที่เป็นทหารหรือตำรวจต้องเป็นคนยังไง

What type of person must a soldier or a policeman be?

    คนที่เป็นทหารหรือตำรวจต้องแข็งแรง

    A person who is soldier or policeman must be strong.

แม่กับพ่อทำงานที่เดียวกัน

My mom and dad work at the same place.

เราเรียนภาษาไทยกับอาจารย์คนเดียวกัน

We study Thai from the same professor.

GRAMMAR

1. ต้อง must, have to

To say, "I must go to school," or "I must study Thai," use **ต้อง** in the pattern below.

S + ต้อง + VP (Verb Phrase)

e.g. เขาต้องเรียนภาษาไทย   He must study Thai.

     เราต้องไปเมืองไทยปีนี้   We have to go to Thailand this year.

Note: To say, "You must not go out," or "You must not talk to him," use **ต้องไม่** in the pattern below.

S + ต้อง + ไม่ + VP

e.g. คุณต้องไม่ไปเที่ยว   You must not go out.

     คุณต้องไม่พูดกับเขา   You must not talk to him.

To say, "You do not have to go to school," or "You don't have to talk to him," use **ไม่ต้อง** instead.

e.g. คุณไม่ต้องไปโรงเรียน   You don't have to go to school.

     คุณไม่ต้องพูดกับเขา   You don't have to talk to him.

2. เพิ่ง just, just now

To say, "He just went to Thailand," or "He just studied Thai," use เพิ่ง in front of the verbs as in the pattern below.

S + เพิ่ง + VP (Verb Phrase)

e.g. เขาเพิ่งไปเมืองไทย   He just went to Thailand.

เขาเพิ่งเรียนภาษาไทย   He just started to study Thai.

3. มานานเท่าไรแล้ว, มานานกี่ปีแล้ว for how long or how many years (has one done something)?

To say, "How long have you been in Thailand?" or "How long have you been married?" use มานานเท่าไรแล้ว or มานานกี่ปีแล้ว at the end of the sentence.

S + SV + มานานเท่าไรแล้ว
มานานกี่ปีแล้ว

e.g. คุณอยู่เมืองไทยมานานเท่าไรแล้ว

How long have you lived in Thailand?

คุณเรียนภาษาไทยมานานกี่ปีแล้ว

How many years have you studied Thai?

4. ที่ which, who, that

ที่ corresponds to the English relative pronouns. It is used to create relative clauses modifying subjects as in these sentences.

S + (ที่ + VP) + VP

e.g. คนที่เป็นอาจารย์เป็นคนไทยหรือเปล่า

Is the person who is a professor Thai?

คนที่ไปเมืองไทยชื่อทอม

The person who went to Thailand is named Tom.

คนที่ไว้ผมยาวเป็นแฟนฉัน

The person with long hair is my girlfriend.

5. Prefix นัก and ช่าง

Some occupations are formed by placing นัก or ช่าง in front of verbs or nouns.

นัก..... functions like the English suffixes –er, –ian, –ist.

e.g. นักพูด   orator, expert speaker

นักเขียน   writer, author

นักเรียน   student

นักบิน   pilot (บิน to fly)

นักร้อง   singer (ร้อง to sing)

นักธุรกิจ   businessman/woman

ช่าง is used in front of verbs or nouns to form noun derivatives, meaning artisan, smith.

e.g. ช่างตัดผม   barber

ช่างทำผม   hairdresser

ช่างถ่ายรูป   photographer

ช่างไม้   carpenter

6. เดียวกัน the same

To say, "We live in the same house," or "We went to the same restaurant," use **เดียวกัน** in this pattern.

S + V + DO + Classifier + เดียวกัน

e.g. เราอยู่บ้านหลังเดียวกัน   We live in the same house.

แม่กับพ่อชอบอาหารอย่างเดียวกัน   My mom and dad like the same kind of food.

เราพักอยู่ที่โรงแรมเดียวกัน   We are staying at the same hotel.

 DRILL

1. เธอทำงานอะไร (a doctor)

   What does she do?

2. เธอทำงานที่ไหน (a hospital)

   Where does she work?

3. เธอเป็นหมอใช่ไหม (yes)

   She is a doctor, right?

4. สามีเธอเป็นอะไร (a teacher)

   What is her husband?

5. เขาเป็นครูที่โรงเรียนไหน (this school)

   He is a teacher at which school?

6. เขาเป็นครูไม่ใช่หรือ (yes)

   He is a teacher, isn't he?

7. พวกเขามีลูกกี่คน (๓)

   How many children do they have?

8. ลูกคนโตของพวกเขาทำงานอะไร (runs a tour company)

   What does their oldest child do?

9. ลูกคนกลางทำงานอะไร (a university student)

   What does their middle child do?

10. แล้วลูกคนเล็กล่ะ (a student)

   What about the youngest one?

11. ครอบครัวนี้เป็นคนไทยใช่ไหม (yes)

   This family is Thai, right?

12. พวกเขาเคยไปประเทศอเมริกาไหม (yes)

   Have they been to the United States?

13. พวกเขาชอบประเทศอเมริกาไหม (yes, very much)

   Did they like America?

14. พวกเขาพักที่ไหน (their friend's house)

   Where did they stay?

15. พวกเขาพักที่โรงแรมใช่ไหม (no)

   They stayed at a hotel, right?

16. พวกเขาชอบอาหารอเมริกันไหม (parents did, but not the children)

   Did they like American food?

PARTNER ACTIVITIES

I. Work with your partner. Look at these pictures and write down the occupations represented.

II. Ask your partner about his or her father/mother (just pick one), using the following questions.

1. พ่อ/แม่คุณ เป็นคนที่ไหน (มาจากไหน)
2. ท่านอายุเท่าไร
3. ท่านทำงานอะไร
4. ท่านเป็นคนยังไง

III. Role Play: TV Interview

You are going to be interviewed by a TV host. Write a conversation between the TV host and yourself, based on the questions below. Then present your role play to the class.

1. คุณทำงานอะไร   What do you do?
2. คุณทำงานที่ไหน   Where do you work?
3. คุณทำงานที่นี่มากี่ปีแล้ว   How many years have you worked here?
4. คุณชอบงานของคุณไหม   Do you like your job?
5. คุณอยากจะเป็นอะไร   What would you like to be?

CLASS ACTIVITIES

I. Using the drawings in Partner Activities, find out information on the person's names, ages, and personality traits from your teacher.

e.g. คนที่เป็นหมอชื่ออะไร
คนที่เป็นหมออายุเท่าไร
คนที่เป็นหมอเป็นคนยังไง

II. Teacher prepares as many cards as there are students and writes an occupation on each card, making sure to make two cards for each occupation. Teacher distributes cards to students. Students circulate around the classroom trying to find the person with the same occupation.

a. ขอโทษนะคะ/ครับ คุณทำงานอะไรคะ/ครับ
b. ดิฉัน/ผมเป็น.....ค่ะ/ครับ

a. ขอโทษนะคะ/ครับ คุณเป็น.....ใช่ไหม
b. ใช่ค่ะ/ครับ or ไม่ใช่ ดิฉัน/ผมไม่ได้เป็น.....ดิฉัน/ผมเป็น.....

III. Occupation Mime: Students write an occupation on a piece of paper and put it in a pile. A student picks a piece of paper and mimes the occupation. Other students guess the occupation. Take turns until all the cards are gone.

EXERCISES

I. Rearrange the dialogue below in a logical order.

................สุดา: ไม่ชอบเลย ฉันอยากเป็นลูกคนโตมากกว่า แล้วเธอล่ะ

................สมชาย: ฉันมีพี่สาว ๒ คน แล้วเธอล่ะ

................สุดา: ฉันสนิทกับพี่สาว แต่ไม่ค่อยสนิทกับพี่ชายเท่าไร

................สมชาย: พี่สาวคนโตเป็นครู คนที่สองทำธุรกิจ

................สุดา: เธอสนิทกับพี่ๆ เธอมั้ย

................สมชาย: ฉันก็เหมือนกัน

................สุดา: พี่สาวฉันเป็นพยาบาล พี่ชายเป็นนักศึกษา แล้วพี่ๆ เธอล่ะ

................สมชาย: เธอชอบเป็นลูกคนเล็กไหม

................สุดา: สมชาย เธอมีพี่น้องกี่คน

................สมชาย: ฉันสนิทกับพี่สาวทั้งสองคน แล้วเธอล่ะ

................สุดา: ฉันมีพี่สาวหนึ่งคน กับพี่ชายหนึ่งคน

................สมชาย: พี่เธอทำงานอะไร

II. Rearrange the words to make sentences.

1. ใช่   *มาลี*   ช่างตัดผม   ไหม   เป็น

2. นักแสดง   เป็น   ไม่   *สมชาย*   ได้

3. ช่างไฟฟ้า   ทั้ง   เป็น   และ   *สมชาย*   ช่างประปา

4. กับ   แม่   ของ   เป็น   พ่อ   ข้าราชการ   เขา

5. ร้านอาหาร   ลูก   ทำงาน   คน   ที่   เล็ก

*The words in italics are names.

CULTURAL CORNER

When the Thais talk to you about jobs or work, they will likely ask you how much you make, a question considered to be impolite by American standards. Thai people are willing to talk about their salary, or how much they paid for this or for that. If you really do not feel comfortable talking about money issues, you can respond with a vague reply (e.g. ไม่มาก not much or ไม่พอ not enough) and then try to change the subject. Or else just be like a Thai—be honest or make it up!!!

Unit 3
Everyday Life

Lesson 10: How Do You Feel?

 คำศัพท์

VERBS

รู้สึก	to feel	โมโห/โกรธ	to be angry
เหนื่อย	to be tired	หงุดหงิด	to be agitated
หิว[ข้าว]	to be hungry	กลุ้มใจ/กังวลใจ	to be worried
หิวน้ำ	to be thirsty	ตกใจ	to get frightened, scared
ง่วงนอน	to be sleepy	งง	to be confused
เบื่อ	to be bored	เสียใจ/เศร้า	to be sad
ร้อน	to be hot	กลัว	to be afraid
หนาว	to be cold	เครียด	to be stressed
		สบายใจ	to be happy

NOUNS

อารมณ์	mood

MISC.

ยังงั้นๆ	so so	เรื่อย ๆ	so so
มากเกินไป	too much	V + [เกิน]ไป	too + SV
เพราะ	because	เลย, จึง	therefore
ไม่ค่อย	not very, hardly	วันนี้	today
ๆ	(ไม้ยมก repetition mark)		

PRONOUN

มัน	it

QUESTION WORD

ทำไม	why

PATTERNS

เป็นยังไง สบายดีหรือ	Hi, how are you?
วันนี้ไม่ค่อยสบาย	I'm not very well today.
ยังงั้นๆ แล้วคุณล่ะ	So so. What about you?
เหมือนกัน	Me too.
(คุณ)เหนื่อยมั้ย/ไหม	Are you tired?
เหนื่อย	Yes, I'm tired.
ไม่เหนื่อย	No, I'm not tired.
คุณง่วงมั้ย/ไหม	Are you sleepy?
นิดหน่อย	A little bit.
หิวข้าวมั้ย/ไหม	Are you hungry?
หิวมาก	I'm very hungry.
หิวนิดหน่อย	I'm a little bit hungry.
หิวจัง(เลย)	I'm really hungry.
ไม่หิวเลย	I'm not hungry at all.
ไม่ค่อยหิว	I'm not very hungry.
วันนี้เขารู้สึกไม่ค่อยสบาย	Today, he doesn't feel well.
ทำไมเขาถึงหิวข้าว	Why is he hungry?
เพราะเขายังไม่ได้กินอะไรเลย	Because he hasn't eaten anything at all.
เขายังไม่ได้กินอะไรเลย เขาเลยหิว	He hasn't eaten anything; therefore, he is hungry.
ทำไมเขาถึงไม่สบาย	Why was she sick?
เขาไม่สบายเพราะเขาทำงาน มาก(เกิน)ไป	She was sick because she worked too much.
เขาทำงานมาก(เกิน)ไป ก็เลย ไม่สบาย	She worked too much so she got sick.
ทำไมเขาถึงไม่กินที่ร้านนี้	Why didn't he eat at this restaurant?
เพราะมันแพงไป	Because it's too expensive.

เมืองไทยร้อนไป เขาเลยไม่อยากไป	Thailand is too hot; therefore, he doesn't want to go.
ฉันชอบซีแอตเติลเพราะไม่หนาวไป	I like Seattle because it is not too cold.
เขาทั้งเหนื่อยทั้งหิวน้ำ	He is both tired and thirsty.
เขาทั้งร้อนทั้งหนาว	She is both hot and cold.
วันนี้เขาอารมณ์ดี	Today he is in good mood.
วันนี้เขาอารมณ์ไม่ดี	Today she is in bad mood.

GRAMMAR

1. ทำไม why

To ask, "Why hasn't he come?" use **ทำไม** in this pattern.

> ทำไม + S + ถึง/จึง + VP (Verb Phrases)

Note: **ถึง** is mostly used in spoken language and **จึง** is used in written form.

e.g. ทำไมเขาถึงไม่ไปเมืองไทย	Why didn't he go to Thailand?
ทำไมพ่อถึงกลุ้มใจ	Why was dad worried?
ทำไมนักเรียนถึงเบื่อ	Why are the students bored?

2. เพราะ because

To answer **ทำไม** question, use conjunction **เพราะ**.

> Sentence + เพราะ + Sentence

e.g. เขาไม่ไปเมืองไทยเพราะเขาไม่มีเงิน

She didn't go to Thailand because she had no money.

พ่อกลุ้มใจเพราะลูกยังไม่กลับบ้าน

Dad is worried because his son is not home yet.

นักเรียนเบื่อเพราะพวกเขาไม่เข้าใจ

The students were bored because they didn't understand.

3. เลย, จึง therefore, so

เลย can also be used to answer **ทำไม** question. See the pattern below (**จึง** is used instead of **เลย** in written language).

> Sentence + Subject + เลย + VP

e.g. เขาไม่มีเงิน(เขา)เลยไม่ไปเมืองไทย
ลูกยังไม่กลับบ้าน พ่อเลยกลุ้มใจ
นักเรียนไม่เข้าใจ เลย เบื่อ

Note: The subject doesn't have to be repeated when it's already established.

4. ไม่ค่อย not very

To say, "It's not very hot," or "She is not very tall," use **ไม่ค่อย** in this pattern.

> S + ไม่ค่อย + Stative Verbs (SV)

e.g. วันนี้เขาไม่ค่อยสบาย   Today he is not very well.
อาหารไม่ค่อยอร่อย   The food is not very delicious.
เขาพูดไทยไม่ค่อยเก่ง   She doesn't speak Thai very well.

5. มาก(เกิน)ไป too much

To say, "I ate too much," or "I talked too much," use **มาก(เกิน)ไป** in this pattern.

> S + VP + มาก(เกิน)ไป

e.g. ฉันกินมากไปเลยไม่หิว   I ate too much so I was not hungry.
เขาพูดมากไปเลยหิวน้ำ   He talked too much so he was thirsty.

6. .....(เกิน)ไป too.....

To say, "The food is too hot," or "This is too expensive," use **(เกิน)ไป** at the end of stative verbs.

> S + SV + ไป

e.g. อาหารเผ็ด(เกิน)ไป   The food is too spicy.
เมืองไทยร้อน(เกิน)ไป   Thailand is too hot.
ปากกาด้ามนี้แพงไป   This pen is too expensive.

7. ทั้ง.....ทั้ง both.....and

To say, "He is both tired and hungry," use the pattern below.

> S + ทั้ง + SV + ทั้ง + SV

e.g. พ่อทั้งใจดีทั้งใจเย็น   My dad is both kind and patient.
แฟนเขาทั้งสวยทั้งดี   His girlfriend is both good and beautiful.

8. ๆ repetition symbol

The symbol ๆ called **ไม้ยมก** means that the word which precedes is repeated. ยังงั้นๆ is read as ยังงั้น ยังงั้น.

This symbol can also be used to create plural nouns. When a Thai says, "เพื่อนมาทานข้าวที่บ้าน," it is not clear how many friends came. It could be one or several. But if he/she says, "เพื่อนๆ มาทานข้าวที่บ้าน," it is then clear that more than one person came to eat at his/her house.

DRILL 1

1. เขาเหนื่อยมั้ย (very much): เขาเหนื่อยมาก   Is he tired?
2. เขาหิวหรือเปล่า (no)   Is he hungry or not?
3. เขาเบื่อมั้ย (not at all)   Is he bored?
4. เขาเหนื่อยหรือเปล่า (not much)   Is he tired or not?
5. เขาหิวมั้ย (a little bit)   Is he hungry?
6. เขาง่วงนอนหรือเปล่า (no, not at all)   Is he sleepy or not?
7. เขาเบื่อหรือเปล่า (very much)   Is he bored or not?

DRILL 2

1. ทำไมเขาถึงไม่ไปโรงเรียน (because she is sick)
   Why didn't she go to school?
2. ทำไมเขาถึงเหนื่อย (because she works too much)
   Why is she tired?
3. ทำไมเขาถึงง่วง (because she hasn't slept)
   Why is she sleepy?
4. ทำไมพ่อถึงโมโห (because his son didn't go to school)
   Why was Dad angry?
5. ทำไมแม่ถึงหงุดหงิด (because Dad was angry)
   Why was Mom agitated?

PARTNER ACTIVITY

Look at these people and decide how they are today.

CLASS ACTIVITIES

I. Feelings Mime: Students write down a feeling on a piece of paper and put it on a pile. A students picks one and acts out the feeling. The class tries to guess the feeling.

II. Teacher makes a set of cards of different feelings, making sure to make at least two cards for each, and distributes cards to students. Students circulate around the classroom to try to find as many people as possible with the same feeling.

III. Vocabulary review: Close your book, and write down as many vocabulary words as you can on a piece of paper. This can be done in groups. Who has the most?

EXERCISES

I. Match cause and effect by drawing connecting lines.

Cause		**Effect**
พี่ชายไม่สบาย		ลูกยังไม่ได้กินข้าว
เขาเหนื่อย		ลูกไม่มาหา
ลุงง่วงนอน		เขาทำงานมาก
น้าไม่ไปทำงาน		เขาไม่สบาย
นักเรียนพูดภาษาไทยเก่ง	เพราะ	พวกเขาขยัน
เขาไม่ค่อยไปกินที่ร้านอาหาร		เขากินมากไป
นักเรียนไม่ง่วงเลย		บ้านเขาไม่มีแอร์คอนดิชั่น
ลูกหิวข้าว		เขาไม่ได้นอน
แม่กลุ้มใจ		เขาไม่มีเงิน
เขาร้อน		อาจารย์สอนเก่ง

II. Then write **ทำไม** questions based on the exercise above and answer the questions with **เลย.**

e.g. ทำไมพี่ชายถึงไม่สบาย
    เขากินมากไปเลยไม่สบาย

1. ....
2. ....
3. ....
4. ....
5. ....
6. ....
7. ....
8. ....
9. ....

Lesson 11: What Are You Doing?

 คำศัพท์

VERBS

พูด	to speak	คุย	to talk, to chat
เดิน	to walk	วิ่ง	to run
อ่านหนังสือ	to read	เขียนหนังสือ	to write
นั่ง	to sit	ยืน	to stand
นอน	to sleep	หาว (นอน)	to yawn
หัวเราะ	to laugh	ร้องไห้	to cry
ดูทีวี	to watch TV	ดื่มน้ำ	to drink
ฟังวิทยุ	to listen to radio	ร้องเพลง	to sing
พักผ่อน	to rest	ฟังเพลง	to listen to music
ทำการบ้าน	to do homework		
พูดโทรศัพท์	to talk on the phone		
โทรไปหา...../ โทรมาหา.....	to call someone e.g. โทรไปหาแม่		

NOUNS

เพลง (เพลง)	song	วิทยุ (เครื่อง)	radio
โทรทัศน์ (เครื่อง)	TV	โทรศัพท์ (เครื่อง)	telephone
การบ้าน	homework		

*Words in parentheses are classifiers.

MISC.

กำลัง	a pre-verb indicating action going on at a given time (v+ing)
กำลังจะ	to be about to (do something)
ยัง.....อยู่	is still doing something
V + กัน	V + to each other

PATTERNS

เขา(กำลัง)ทำอะไร	What is she doing?
เขา(กำลัง)ดูทีวี	She is watching TV.
กินข้าว	She is eating (a meal).
อ่านหนังสือ	She is reading.
เขาทำอะไร	What is she doing?
เขายังดูทีวีอยู่	She is still watching TV.
เขายังกินข้าวอยู่	She is still eating.
เขายังอ่านหนังสืออยู่	She is still reading.
เขากำลังจะไปโรงเรียน	He is about to go to school.
ฉันกำลังจะโทรไปหาคุณ	I'm about to call you.
เขาทั้งอ่านหนังสือทั้งดูทีวี	He is both reading and watching TV.
เขาทั้งหัวเราะทั้งร้องไห้	He is laughing and crying (at the same time).
เขากำลังคุยกัน	They are talking.

GRAMMAR

1. กำลัง

To express the present or past continuous, e.g., "They were talking on the phone," or "He is eating," use this pattern.

S + กำลัง + VP + (อยู่)

e.g. เขากำลังดูทีวี	He is watching TV.
เขากำลังนอน	He is sleeping.

2. กำลังจะ

To say, "I'm about to go to school," or "He was about to eat," use this pattern.

S + กำลังจะ + VP

e.g. ผมกำลังจะไปนอน	I'm about to go to bed.
เขากำลังจะกลับบ้าน	He was about to go home.

Note: Neither **กำลัง** nor **กำลังจะ** can be used in negative form.

3. ยัง.....อยู่

To say, "She is still doing her homework," or "He is still a student," use **ยัง.....อยู่** in this pattern.

S + ยัง + VP + อยู่

e.g. เขายังนอนอยู่   He is still sleeping.

เขายังเป็นอาจารย์สอนภาษาไทยอยู่ที่นี่   She is still a Thai professor here.

4. V + กัน V to each other

A verb followed by **กัน** is used to imply a plural subject. It means "doing something to each other."

S + VP + กัน

e.g. เขาคุยกัน   They talk (to each other).

เขาพูดโทรศัพท์กัน   They talk on the phone.

เขาไม่ชอบกัน   They dislike each other.

ลูกตีกัน   The children hit each other.

พ่อกับแม่ทะเลาะกัน   Mom and Dad quarrel.

DRILL

1. ทอมกำลังทำอะไร (talking on the phone)   What is Tom doing?
2. เจนกำลังทำอะไร (writing)   What is Jane doing?
3. จอนกำลังทำอะไร (eating)   What is John doing?
4. ลูกๆ กำลังทำอะไร (watching TV)   What are the kids doing?
5. พ่อกำลังทำอะไร (reading)   What is Dad doing?
6. ตากำลังทำอะไร (listening to music)   What is Grandfather doing?
7. ยายกำลังทำอะไร (sleeping)   What is Grandmother doing?

PARTNER ACTIVITY

Look at these people in the picture and write down what they are doing.

CLASS ACTIVITIES

I. Using the same picture, the teacher makes up occupations, names, and/or ages for each person in the picture. Students find out all the information by asking these questions.

คนที่กำลังเดินชื่ออะไร
คนที่กำลังเดินทำงานอะไร
คนที่กำลังเดินอายุเท่าไร

II. Mime: Write down an activity on a piece of paper and put it in a pile. A student picks one and acts it out, asking, ผม/ดิฉันกำลังทำอะไร. The class tries to guess the activity.

To make it more challenging, the teacher can write down a series of activities on a piece of paper. A student has to mime all the activities in sequence. The rest of the class guesses the activities.

EXERCISES

I. Complete the story below by filling in the blanks with the words given.

ทั้งสอง	ที่	อยู่	อาชีพ	ภริยา	และ
แล้วก็	คน	ไม่ค่อย	อายุ	ไว้	

นิคมมี...............เป็นอาจารย์ เขาสอนภาษาไทย...............มหาวิทยาลัยวอชิงตัน นิคม
...............ที่อเมริกามาได้ ๑๕ ปีแล้ว .... ของเขาเป็นคนเอมริกัน ....มีลูก
๓ คน เป็นผู้หญิงสองคน และผู้ชายหนึ่งคน

นิคม...............๓๕ ปี เขาเป็นคนผอมและสูง ไม่...............หนวด เครา นิคมเป็น ....ใจดี
และพูดเก่ง วันนี้นิคม...............สบาย เขาเลย...............บ้านอ่านหนังสือ...............นอนพักผ่อน

*Some words can be used more than once.

Then make up questions from the story above and answer them.

1. ....
2. ....
3. ....
4. ....
5. ....

II. Fill in the blanks.

1. ทั้งฉัน...............เขาไม่สบายวันนี้

2. คุณ...............ทำอะไรอยู่

3. ฉันไม่เหนื่อย............... แล้วคุณ...............

4. เขาพูดไทยไม่...............เก่ง พี่ชายเขาพูดเก่ง...............เขา

5. เขาชอบทานข้าว...............ร้านอาหาร

6. เขาอยู่...............

7. คน...............ชื่ออะไร

8. ลูก...............แรกชื่ออะไรนะ

9. เขากำลังนอน...............ทำงาน

Lesson 12: Hobbies
Likes and Dislikes

 คำศัพท์

NOUNS

เวลา	time	งานอดิเรก (อย่าง)	hobby
รถ (คัน)	car	หนัง (เรื่อง)	movie

*Words in parentheses are classifiers.

VERBS

ว่าง	to be free
เล่น	to play (music, musical instruments, or sports)
เล่นบาสเก็ตบอล	to play basketball
เล่นฟุตบอล	to play soccer
เล่นสกี	to ski
เล่นสเก็ต	to skate
เล่นดนตรี	to play musical instruments
เล่นกีตาร์	to play guitar
เล่นเปียโน	to play piano
ดูหนัง	to watch movies
ดูวิดีโอ	to watch videos
เต้นรำ	to dance
ขี่จักรยาน	to ride a bike
ซื้อของ	to shop
ว่ายน้ำ	to swim
ออกกำลังกาย	to exercise
ไปเดินเล่น	to go out for a walk
ไปงานเลี้ยง[งานปาร์ตี้]	to go to a party
ไปเที่ยว	to go out and about
ไปทานข้าวนอกบ้าน	to eat out
ขับรถ[ไป]เที่ยว	to drive around

PRE-VERBS

มักจะ	tend to, like to
ไม่ค่อย	hardly, rarely, seldom

MISC.

ถ้า.....ก็	if
แล้วก็	then (sentence connector)
V + เป็น/ไม่เป็น	know how to/don't know how to
บ่อย	often

PATTERNS

คุณชอบทำอะไรบ้าง ถ้ามีเวลาว่าง

What do you like to do if you have free time?

ถ้ามีเวลาว่าง ดิฉัน/ผมชอบเล่นกีฬา เล่นเปียโน หรือ ไปซื้อของ

If I have free time, I like to play sports, play the piano, or go shopping.

คุณมักจะทำอะไร ถ้ามีเวลาว่าง

What do you tend to do if you have free time?

ถ้ามีเวลาว่าง ดิฉัน/ผมมักจะไปเที่ยวกับเพื่อนๆ

If I have time, I tend to go out with friends.

คุณมีงานอดิเรกอะไรบ้าง

What are your hobbies?

ดิฉัน/ผมชอบอ่านหนังสือ เล่นกีตาร์ แล้วก็ดูหนัง

I like to read, play guitar, and watch movies.

ดิฉัน/ผมชอบขี่จักรยาน เล่นฟุตบอล แล้วก็ฟังเพลง

I like to ride my bike, play soccer, and listen to music.

ดิฉัน/ผมชอบเล่นกีฬา และขับรถเที่ยว

I like to play sports and drive around.

(คุณ)ชอบเล่นกีฬามั้ย

Do you like to play sports?

ชอบเล่นกีฬาแต่ไม่ชอบเล่นเทนนิส

I like to play sports but I don't like to play tennis.

ไม่ชอบเล่นกีฬา แต่ชอบออกกำลังกาย

I do not like to play sports but I like to exercise.

(คุณ)ชอบเล่นดนตรีมั้ย

Do you like to play musical instruments?

ชอบเล่นดนตรี แต่เล่นเปียโนไม่เป็น

I like to play musical instruments but I don't know how to play piano.

(คุณ)เล่นเปียโนเป็นมั้ย	Do you know how to play piano?
เล่นเป็น แต่ไม่เก่ง	Yes I do, but not very well.
เล่นไม่ค่อยเป็น	I don't play very well.

ดิฉัน/ผมไม่ค่อยไปซื้อของ	I hardly go shopping.
ออกกำลังกาย	I hardly exercise.
ทานข้าวนอกบ้าน	I hardly eat out.
ไปดูหนัง	I hardly go to see a movie.

ดิฉัน/ผมไปซื้อของบ่อยๆ	I go shopping often.
ออกกำลังกายบ่อยๆ	I exercise often.
ทานข้าวนอกบ้านบ่อยๆ	I eat out often.
ดูหนังบ่อยๆ	I go to see a movie often.

เขาไปทานข้าวแล้วเขาก็ไปดูหนัง	He ate out and then went to see a movie.

GRAMMAR

1. เป็น, ไม่เป็น

To say, "I can do it (because I know how)," use this pattern.

$$S + VP + เป็น$$

To say, "I cannot do something (because I do not know how)," use this pattern.

$$S + VP + ไม่เป็น$$

e.g. ฉันเล่นกีตาร์เป็นแต่เล่นเปียโนไม่เป็น

I know how to play guitar but not piano.

เขาเล่นสกีเป็นแต่เล่นสเก็ตไม่เป็น

He knows how to ski but not how to skate.

To ask the question, "Do you know how to .....?" use these patterns.

S + VP + เป็น + ไหม

e.g. คุณเล่นกีตาร์เป็นไหม

Do you know how to play guitar?

Answer	Yes:	V + เป็น	Yes, I do.
	No:	V + ไม่เป็น	No, I don't.

Verb + ได้/ไม่ได้ has a broader meaning than Verb + เป็น/ไม่เป็น. When someone says, เล่นสกีไม่ได้ (I can't ski), it could be because he/she doesn't know how, has no time, or is not physically up to it, etc.

2. ถ้า if

As in English, ถ้า can appear at the beginning of two independent clauses or in between them.

ถ้า + Sentence + S + (ก็)จะ + VP

S + จะ + VP + ถ้า + Sentence

e.g. ถ้าเขาไม่มา ผมก็จะกลับบ้าน

If he doesn't come, then I will go home.

ผมจะกลับบ้าน ถ้าเขาไม่มา

I will go home if she doesn't come.

คุณมักจะทำอะไรถ้ามีเวลาว่าง

What do you usually do if you have free time?

ถ้ามีเวลาว่าง ผมมักจะไปดูหนังกับเพื่อนๆ

If I have free time, I tend to go see movies with friends.

3. แล้วก็ then (word and sentence connector)

To say something like, "She is tired, sleepy, and hungry," use แล้วก็ as a word connector.

e.g. เขาชอบอาหารไทย อาหารจีน แล้วก็อาหารเกาหลี

I like Thai, Chinese, and Korean food.

ถ้ามีเวลาว่าง ฉันชอบไปซื้อของ ไปดูหนัง แล้วก็ไปเที่ยวกับเพื่อน

If I have free time, I like to go shopping, see movies, and go out with friends.

แล้วก็ can also be used as sentence connector. To say something like, "She went shopping and then she went out for a meal," use this pattern.

$$S + VP + แล้ว + (Pronoun) + ก็ + VP$$

e.g. เขาไปซื้อของแล้ว(เขา)ก็ไปหาเพื่อน

She went shopping and then she visited her friend.

เขาไปเรียนหนังสือ แล้วก็ไปว่ายน้ำ

He went to school and then he went for a swim.

4. ไม่ค่อย hardly, rarely, seldom

To say, "I hardly cook," or "I seldom eat out," use ไม่ค่อย in this pattern.

$$S + ไม่ค่อย + VP$$

e.g. เขาไม่ค่อยพูดกับฉัน   She hardly speaks to me.

เขาไม่ค่อยออกกำลังกาย   He hardly exercises.

Note: When ไม่ค่อย is used with stative verbs, it means "not very" (see lesson 10). For example, เขาไม่ค่อยสูง (He is not very tall) or ครูไม่ค่อยดุ (His teacher is not very strict).

5. บ่อย often

To say, "I eat Thai food often," or "She often goes to Thailand," use บ่อย as in the pattern below.

$$S + VP + บ่อย$$

On the contrary, to say, "I don't eat Thai food very often," or "She doesn't go to Thailand very often," use ไม่บ่อย instead.

$$S + VP + ไม่บ่อย$$

To form a question, use question tag บ่อยไหม

e.g. เขาไปเมืองไทยบ่อยไหม   Does he go to Thailand often?

    บ่อย   Yes, he does.

    ไม่บ่อย   No, he doesn't.

    คุณกินอาหารไทยบ่อยไหม   Do you eat Thai food often?

      ผม/ดิฉันกินอาหารไทยบ่อยมาก   Yes, I eat Thai food very often.

6. มักจะ tend to

To say, "I tend to stay home," use **มักจะ** in front of verbs.

S + มักจะ   + VP

e.g. ฉันมักจะพูดไทยกับเขา   I tend to speak Thai to him.

พ่อมักจะไปดูหนังกับแม่   Dad tends to go see movies with Mom.

SUBSTITUTION DRILLS

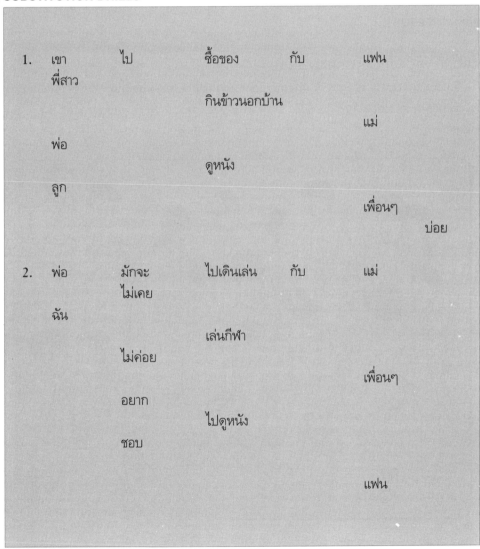

1. เขา   ไป   ซื้อของ   กับ   แฟน
    พี่สาว

                         กินข้าวนอกบ้าน

                                               แม่

    พ่อ

                         ดูหนัง

    ลูก

                                               เพื่อนๆ
                                                       บ่อย

2. พ่อ   มักจะ   ไปเดินเล่น   กับ   แม่
              ไม่เคย

    ฉัน

                         เล่นกีฬา

    ไม่ค่อย

                                               เพื่อนๆ

    อยาก   ไปดูหนัง

    ชอบ

                                                   แฟน

PARTNER ACTIVITY

Ask your partner these questions, then report your findings to the class.

1. ถ้าคุณมีเวลาว่าง คุณมักจะทำอะไรบ้าง
2. มีอะไรบ้างที่คุณไม่ชอบหรือไม่เคยทำ

CLASS ACTIVITY

Mime: Students write down an activity on a piece of paper and put it in a pile. A student picks one and follows the instructions and asks ผม/ดิฉันกำลังทำอะไร. The class guesses the activity.

GROUP VOCABULARY CHALLENGE

Students work in groups of three or four and talk about what they usually do during weekends or at school break. Make a list with your group. Read your group's list to the class.

III. Group Survey: Forming new groups, ask everyone in your group these questions to find out if he/she likes to do the following things when he/she has free time. Check **มักจะ** or **ไม่ค่อย**. Then report your group's results to the class.

ถ้าคุณมีเวลาว่าง คุณ	มักจะ	ไม่ค่อย
1. ดูทีวี	....	....
2. ไปดูหนัง	....	....
3. เล่นดนตรี	....	....
4. เต้นรำ	....	....
5. เล่นกีฬา	....	....
6. ออกกำลังกาย	....	....
7. ไปซื้อของ	....	....
8. ว่ายน้ำ	....	....

EXERCISES

I. Read the story below. Then answer the following questions. Make up your own question and answer in no. 6.

ถ้ามีเวลาว่าง นิคมมักจะไปเล่นกีฬา เขาชอบเล่นกีฬาหลายอย่าง เช่น บาสเก็ตบอล ฟุตบอล ว่ายน้ำ แล้วก็เทนนิส ถ้าไม่ไปเล่นกีฬา นิคมก็จะไปออกกำลังกายที่โรงยิม

ภริยาของเขาชอบไปดูหนังและซื้อของ ถ้ามีเวลาว่าง เธอเล่นกีฬาไม่เป็นเลย

ถ้าทั้งสองมีเวลาว่าง พวกเขามักจะพาลูกๆ ไปทานข้าวนอกบ้านแล้วก็ไปดูกีฬา หรือไปดูหนัง ลูกๆ ของเขาชอบไปดูหนังมากกว่าไปดูกีฬา

1. นิคมเล่นกีฬาอะไรเป็นบ้าง
2. ถ้าไม่ไปเล่นกีฬา นิคมมักจะทำอะไรถ้ามีเวลาว่าง
3. ภริยาของเขาชอบเล่นกีฬาเหมือนนิคมใช่ไหม
4. ถ้ามีเวลาว่าง ภริยานิคมชอบทำอะไร
5. ลูกๆ ของเขาชอบดูกีฬามากกว่าดูหนังใช่ไหม
6. ....

II. Translate these sentences into Thai.

1. Do you know how to play piano?

2. I know how to play piano, but not guitar.

3. I know how to play piano, but not very well.

4. I will go home if he doesn't want to see a movie with me.

5. They went shopping and then they went to a Japanese restaurant.

6. I hardly eat out.

7. That movie is not very good.

Lesson 13: Invitations and Excuses

((•)) คำศัพท์

NOUNS

ธุระ	errand
นัด	appointment

VERBS

ชวน	to invite (informal)
เชิญ	to invite (formal)
ขอตัว	to be excused (from a gathering)
รอ/คอย	to wait
ไม่เป็นไร	never mind

MISC.

ตอนนี้, เดี๋ยวนี้	now
เดี๋ยว	a few moments
พรุ่งนี้	tomorrow
ประเดี๋ยวเดียว	a moment
อาจจะ	might
ด้วยกัน	together
ด้วย	also, in addition to
ถ้างั้น..... (ก็แล้วกัน)	in that case, if so
QW + ก็ได้	.....ever
ขอ	May I.....?
เยอะ	a lot (colloquial)
ก็ได้, ก็ดี	O.K.

PARTICLES

นะ, เถอะ, เถอะนะ, เถอะน่า, ซิ insistence particles

หรอก a particle often used with ไม่

((•))) PATTERNS

(เรา) ไปซื้อของ(ด้วย)กันไหม

Shall we go shopping (together)?

> ขอโทษนะ ดิฉัน/ผมมีธุระ/นัด ไปไม่ได้

> ขอโทษนะ ดิฉัน/ผมติดธุระ/นัด ไปไม่ได้

> Sorry, I have other engagements. (I) can't.

> ขอโทษด้วย ดิฉัน/ผมไม่ว่าง

> I'm sorry, I'm not free.

> คุณไปเถอะ ดิฉัน/ผมเพิ่งไป(ซื้อของ)มา

> (You) Go ahead. I just went (shopping).

ไปเที่ยวกันมั้ย

Shall we go out?

> ยังไปไม่ได้ เดี๋ยวค่อยไปได้มั้ย

> I can't go yet. Can we go later?

> ตอนนี้ยังไม่ว่าง ไปพรุ่งนี้ได้มั้ย

> I'm not free now. Can we go tomorrow?

> ขอโทษ ดิฉัน/ผมมีการบ้านต้องทำ

> Sorry, I have homework to do.

> ขอโทษ ดิฉัน/ผมต้องไปทำงาน

> Sorry, I have to go to work.

ไปดูหนังเรื่องนี้ด้วยกันมั้ย

Shall we go see this movie together?

> เรื่องนี้ดูแล้ว ไปดูเรื่องนั้นดีกว่า

> I've seen this one. Let's go see that movie.

ไปดูหนังเรื่องไหนดี

Which movie would be good to go see?

> เรื่องไหนก็ได้

> Any movie will do.

(เรา)ไปเต้นรำกันมั้ย

Shall we go dancing?

> เต้นรำไม่เป็น ต้องขอตัวด้วย

> I don't know how to dance. I'll have to pass.

112

ไปกินข้าวกันนะ

Let's go eat out.

 คุณไปเถอะ ดิฉัน/ผมยังไม่หิว

 You go ahead. I'm not hungry yet.

(เรา)ไปกินอาหารจีนกันดีไหม

Shall we go have Chinese food? (Will it be a good idea?)

 ดีเหมือนกัน

 Yes (sounds like a good idea)

 ไปซิ

 Yes, let's go.

 ไม่อยากกินอาหารจีน ไปกินอาหารไทยดีกว่า

 I don't want to eat Chinese. I'd rather go have Thai food.

ไปกินข้าวด้วยกันมั้ย

Shall we go eat?

 อยากไป แต่ตอนนี้ไม่มีเวลา

 I would like to go but I don't have time now.

ไปเถอะ ประเดี๋ยวเดียวเท่านั้น

Come on! It won't take long.

 แต่ดิฉัน/ผมมีงานเยอะ

 But I have a lot of work.

เถอะน่า ไปไม่นานหรอก

Come on. Let's go! It won't take long.

 ไปก็ไป

 O.K.

อยากไปซื้อของด้วยกันมั้ย

Would you like to go shopping together?

 ดีเหมือนกัน

 Good idea!

ไปดูหนังกันมั้ย

Shall we go see a movie?

ขอโทษ มีนัดแล้ว

Sorry, I already have an appointment.

ถ้างั้น ไปดูหนังพรุ่งนี้มั้ย

In that case, shall we go tomorrow?

พรุ่งนี้ ดิฉัน/ผมก็ไม่ว่าง(เหมือนกัน)

I'm not free tomorrow either.

ไม่เป็นไร ถ้างั้น เอาไว้นัดกันอีกที ก็แล้วกัน

Never mind. In that case, let's set up another time, then (we'll take that up later).

ถ้างั้น ดิฉัน/ผมไปก่อนนะ

In that case, I'll be going now.

อยากชวนคุณไปทานข้าวด้วยกัน คุณว่างไหม

I would like to invite you out for a meal. Are you free?

ว่างค่ะ/ครับ ขอบคุณ

Yes, thank you.

ถ้างั้น ไปกันเลยดีมั้ย คุณอยากทานอะไร

In that case, should we go now? What would you like to eat?

อะไรก็ได้ค่ะ/ครับ

Whatever you offer (anything will do).

เขาอาจจะไปดูหนังกับเรา

He might go see a movie with us.

ไปปาร์ตี้กันเถอะ	Let's go party!
ตกลง	O.K.
ไปก็ไป	O.K.
ไปก็ได้	O.K.
ไปก็ดี	O.K. (sounds good)
ไปซิ	Let's go.

ขอไปดูหนังด้วยได้มั้ย	May I go see the movie with you?
ได้ซิ	You can, of course.

GRAMMAR

1. กัน, ด้วยกัน together

As in **กัน** (to each other), **ด้วยกัน** implies a plural subject. It simply means "doing something together." **ด้วยกัน** is sometimes shortened to **กัน**

S + VP + ด้วยกัน

e.g.	เขาไปหาอาจารย์ด้วยกัน	They went to see the professor together.
	พ่อกับแม่ไปเมืองไทยด้วยกัน	Mom and dad went to Thailand together.
	อยากไปดูหนังด้วยกันมั้ย	Would you like to go see a movie together?

2. ด้วย also (in addition to)

Unlike **ด้วยกัน**, **ด้วย** doesn't necessarily imply a plural subject. See examples below.

e.g. ฉันอยากไปดูหนังด้วย

I would like to go see a movie (with you) also.

ฉันชอบอาหารไทย เขาก็ชอบอาหารไทยด้วย

I like Thai food. He also likes Thai food.

เขาไปซื้อของแล้วก็ไปดูหนังด้วย

She went shopping and then went to see a movie as well.

3. ได้, ไม่ได้ can, can't

To make an expression like, "I can (do something because circumstances make it possible or I know how to)," use this pattern.

S + VP + ได้

To say, "I can't," use this pattern.

S + VP + ไม่ได้

e.g. ฉันไปดูหนังกับคุณได้

I can go see a movie with you (have time).

ฉันเล่นเปียโนได้

I can play piano (know how to and/or have time).

ฉันพูดไทยได้

I can speak Thai (know how to)

ฉันไปดูหนังกับคุณไม่ได้

I can't go see a movie with you (have no time and/or am not free).

ฉันเล่นเปียโนไม่ได้

I can't play piano (don't know how and/or don't have time).

115

ฉันพูดไทยไม่ได้

I can't speak Thai (don't know how).

To ask a "can" question, just add any yes/no question words at the end of the sentence. Invitations with "ได้ไหม, ได้หรือเปล่า" question tags are less insistent than invitations with นะ, เถอะ, etc. particles (see 4 below).

ไปดูหนังด้วยได้ไหม   Can I go see a movie (with you)?

Yes: ได้/ได้ซิ   Yes, of course.

No: ไม่ได้   No, I can't.

ไปซื้อของกับคุณได้หรือเปล่า

Can I go shopping with you?

Yes: ได้/ได้ซิ

No: ไม่ได้

เราไปด้วยกันได้ใช่ไหม

We can go together, right?

Yes: ใช่

No: ไม่ใช่

4. มั้ย, นะ, เถอะ, เถอะนะ, เถอะน่า, ซิ insistent sentence final particles

When extending an invitation, a person has a choice to be or not to be insistent. He can use ไหม, a yes/no question word, thus giving the listener the choice of accepting or declining an invitation.

One can vary degree of insistence by using มั้ย, นะ, เถอะ, เถอะนะ, เถอะน่า, ซิ at the end of the sentence. The following patterns show the different degrees of insistence in an ascending order.

ไปทานข้าวด้วยกันมั้ย

ไปทานข้าวด้วยกันนะ

ไปทานข้าวด้วยกันเถอะ

ไปทานข้าวด้วยกันเถอะนะ

ไปทานข้าวด้วยกันเถอะน่า

ไปทานข้าวด้วยกันซิ

5. ก็ได้, ก็ดี, ซิ

When accepting an invitation or when asked to make a choice, a person can choose one of the following patterns, which different degrees of enthusiasm.

Verb or Noun + ก็ได้
ก็ดี
ซิ

e.g. ไปเที่ยวเมืองไทยกันมั้ย Shall we go to Thailand together?

ไปก็ไป	O.K.
ไปก็ได้	O.K.
ไปก็ดี	O.K. Sounds good.
ไปซิ	Let's go.

คุณอยากทานอะไร	What would you like to eat?
อะไรก็ได้	Anything will do.
อาหารไทยก็ได้	Thai food is O.K.
อาหารไทยก็ดี	Thai food sounds good.
อาหารจีนซิ	Chinese food, of course.

6. ขอ May I have ....., may I.....

To ask for permission or make a request like, "May I go with you?"or "May I have some water?" use **ขอ** at the beginning of the sentence. The word **หน่อย** or **นะ** are often placed at the end to soften the request. It can also be made into a yes/no question by using the **ได้ไหม** question tag, thus giving the listener a chance to decline.

e.g. ขอไปเที่ยวด้วยได้ไหม	Might I go with you?
ขอไปด้วยคนนะ	May I go with you?
ขอใช้โทรศัพท์หน่อยนะ	May I use your phone?
ขอข้าวหน่อย	May I have some rice?
ขอโค้กหน่อย	May I have some Coke?

7. หรอก

A particle often used with statements of negation, contradiction, or those correcting a misunderstanding.

e.g. ไปนานไหม

Are we going to go for a long time?

ไม่นานหรอก

No, we are not (assurance)

นี่แพงจัง

This is very expensive.

ไม่แพงหรอก

No, it is not (contradiction).

นี่คุณจอห์นใช่ไหม

This is Mr. John, right?

ไม่ใช่หรอก

No, he is not (correct misunderstanding).

DRILL 1: V + ก็ได้, N + ก็ได้

1. จะไปด้วยกันไหม

Would you like to go together?

ไปด้วยกันก็ได้

O.K.

2. ไปกินข้าวไหม

Would you like to go eat?

3. จะกลับหรือยัง

Would you like to go home?

4. จะไปหาเพื่อนไหม

Would you want to visit friends?

5. ไปดูหนังเรื่องนี้ไหม

Would you like to go see this movie?

6. อยากไปกับเขาไหม

Would you like to go with her?

7. จะทานอะไรดี อาหารไทย หรือ อาหารจีน

What would you like to eat? Thai or Chinese?

8. จะพักที่ไหนดี โรงแรมนี้ หรือ โรงแรมนั้น

Where should we stay? This hotel or that hotel?

9. จะไปประเทศไหนดี ประเทศญี่ปุ่น หรือเกาหลี

Which country should we go to? Japan or Korea?

10. จะทำอะไรดี ไปกินข้าวหรือไปดูหนัง

What would you like to do? Eat out or go to a movie?

DRILL 2: QW + ก็ได้

1. คุณอยากไปกับใคร

   With whom would you like to go?

   ไปกับใครก็ได้

   With whomever.

2. คุณอยากจะทานอะไร

   What would you like to eat?

3. คุณอยากไปหาใคร

   Whom would you like to visit?

4. คุณอยากไปเที่ยวที่ไหน

   Where would you like to go?

5. คุณอยากทำอะไร

   What would you like to do?

6. คุณอยากอ่านหนังสือเล่มไหน

   Which book would you like to read?

7. คุณอยากไปกินข้าวร้านไหน

   Which restaurant would you like to go to?

8. คุณอยากไปดูหนังกับใคร

   Whom would you like to see the movie with?

9. คุณอยากไปดูหนังเรื่องไหน

   Which movie would you like to see?

10. คุณจะใส่รองเท้าคู่ไหน

    Which pair of shoes are you going to wear?

PARTNER ACTIVITIES

I. Work with a partner. Take turns giving invitations using the following verb phrases. Vary the degree of your insistence. Also practice accepting an invitation. Some students can demonstrate it in front of the class.

ไปเที่ยว	ทานอาหารเกาหลี	ไปเล่นเทนนิส
ดูหนัง	ดูกีฬา	ไปงานเลี้ยง

II. Changing Sentences: Make up five sentences using the words provided below. Then share your sentences with your classmates.

Subjects	Pre-verbs	Verbs	Objects
เขา	ไม่ค่อย	ไปหา	อาหารเผ็ดๆ
เด็กๆ	มักจะ	อยู่	ปู่ย่าตายาย
พ่อแม่	ต้อง	ไป	ภาษาจีน
นักเรียน	เคย	มาหา	เพื่อน
เพื่อนๆ	อยาก	กิน	เปียโน
พี่สาว	ไม่เคย	ดื่ม	งานเลี้ยง
ลุง	ชอบ	คุยกับ	โรงแรม
พ่อแม่		พักที่	เบียร์
		เรียน	โรงเรียน
		เล่น	น้ำร้อน
		อยู่	เมืองไทย
			บ้าน

CLASS ACTIVITIES

I. Teacher asks students to come up with as many excuses as they can, writing them all on the board, and then erasing them. Students divide into groups of three or four and write down as many excuses as they can. Which group has the most?

ฉันไปกับคุณไม่ได้เพราะ...

II. Teacher prepares as many cards as there are students and writes a hobby on each card, making sure to make at least two cards for each hobby. Teacher distributes cards to students. Students find the person who shares their hobby by inviting others to go do the activity on the card. The invitee can accept the invitation only if he/she has the same hobby; otherwise, he/she has to decline the invitation politely, with an excuse.

EXERCISES

1. Reading Comprehension

Read this passage, then answer the questions in *complete sentences*.

คุณจอห์นเป็นคนอเมริกันมาอยู่เมืองไทยได้นานแล้ว   เขาสอนภาษาอังกฤษที่เมืองไทย   คุณ
จอห์นเป็นโสด   ยังไม่ได้แต่งงาน   เขามีเพื่อนคนไทยหลายคน   แต่มีเพื่อนผู้หญิงไทย ๒-๓ คน
เท่านั้น   คุณจอห์นชอบอยู่ที่เมืองไทยมาก   เพราะอาหารถูกและอร่อย   แต่เขาทานเผ็ดมากไม่ได้
คุณจอห์นพูดไทยเก่งมากแต่อ่านเขียนไม่ได้เลย ตอนนี้เขากำลังเรียนภาษาไทยอยู่ ถ้ามีเวลาว่าง
จอห์นชอบฟังเพลงไทยและไปดูหนังกับเพื่อนๆ   ถ้ามีเวลาว่างมาก   เขาชอบไปเที่ยวต่างจังหวัด
หรือกลับไปหาพ่อแม่ที่อเมริกา

1. คุณจอห์นมาจากประเทศไหน
2. เขาอยู่เมืองไทยนานแล้วหรือยัง
3. เขาแต่งงานแล้วหรือยัง
4. เขามีเพื่อนผู้หญิงไทยหลายคนใช่ไหม
5. ทำไมเขาถึงชอบเมืองไทย
6. เขาพูดภาษาไทยเก่งไหม แล้วอ่านเขียนล่ะ
7. ถ้ามีเวลาว่างนิดหน่อย จอห์นชอบทำอะไร
8. ถ้ามีเวลาว่างมาก เขาชอบไปไหน
9. แล้วคุณล่ะ ถ้าคุณมีเวลาว่างคุณชอบทำอะไร

II. Give responses to these invitations.

1. ไปทานข้าวด้วยกันมั้ย

    accept: ....

    decline: ....

2. เธอว่างมั้ย ไปดูหนังกันมั้ย

    accept: ....

    decline: ....

3. เย็นนี้ไปทานข้าวที่บ้านฉันมั้ย

    accept: ....

    decline: ....

CULTURAL NOTES

When Thai people extend an invitation, it is a gesture of friendship and a wish to have a closer relationship. Thais tend to decline an invitation when first extended so as not to trouble the inviter. The feeling of reluctance and the desire not to trouble others is called เกรงใจ. The inviter has to be insistent in order to show his/her sincerity. When one really wants to decline an invitation, one needs to qualify that negative answer with adequate justification; otherwise, it will be interpreted as a rejection. Thais tend to accept invitations in order to avoid hurting others' feelings, except among close friends or family, when declining an invitation can be acceptable.

This custom often seems to confuse foreigners, who are more familiar with direct responses ("no means no"). When a Thai is invited for a meal, he/she will decline when more food is offered so as not to trouble the host, i.e. make the host cook or order more food). It is the host's job to insist upon having more to eat. So in certain circumstances, a "no" doesn't always mean no!

Insistence is more common in Thai culture, and Thai people may adjust their behavior accordingly, turning down the first invitation in the knowledge that the inviting party will probably insist.

Lesson 14: Daily Routine

 คำศัพท์

VERBS

ตื่นนอน	to get up	นอนกลางวัน/นอนเล่น	to nap
อาบน้ำ	to bathe	เข้านอน	to go to bed
สระผม	to wash one's hair	รีบ	to hurry
หวีผม	to comb one's hair	อ่าน	to read
โกนหนวด	to shave	เช็ค	to check
แปรงฟัน	to brush one's teeth		
แต่งตัว	to dress		
ทำการบ้าน	to do homework		

PRE-VERB

ควร, ควรจะ	should

NOUNS

อาหารเช้า (มื้อ)	breakfast	กาแฟ (แก้ว, ถ้วย)	coffee
อาหารกลางวัน (มื้อ)	lunch	ชา (แก้ว, ถ้วย)	tea
อาหารเย็น (มื้อ)	dinner	นม (แก้ว)	milk
อาหารว่าง (มื้อ)	snack	หนังสือพิมพ์ (ฉบับ)	newspaper
		อีเมล์ (ข้อความ, ฉบับ)	e-mail
สบู่ (ก้อน, ขวด)	soap	แชมพู (ขวด)	shampoo
ยาสีฟัน (หลอด)	toothpaste	ผ้าเช็ดตัว (ผืน)	towel
แปรงสีฟัน (อัน)	toothbrush		

*Words in parentheses are classifiers.

MISC.

ทุก, ทุกๆ	every	วันเว้นวัน	every other day
วัน	day	ตามปกติ	normally
ทุกวัน	everyday	ไม่ได้	negative "past tense"
ก่อน	before		
หลัง	after		
เสร็จ	to finish or to be done with something		

PATTERNS

ตามปกติเขาอาบน้ำและสระผมทุกวัน

Normally he bathes and shampoos everyday.

ตามปกติ ตื่นนอนแล้ว คุณทำอะไรบ้าง

Normally what do you do after getting up?

> ดิฉัน/ผมดื่มกาแฟ อ่านหนังสือพิมพ์ เช็คอีเมล์ อาบน้ำแล้วก็ไปโรงเรียน
>
> I drink coffee, read the newspaper, check e-mail, have a bath, and then go to school.

คุณไม่ทานข้าวก่อนไปโรงเรียนหรือ

Don't you eat before going to school?

> ดิฉัน/ผมไม่ค่อยได้กินอาหารเช้า
>
> I hardly get to eat breakfast.

วันนี้เขาสระผมหรือเปล่า

Did she wash her hair today?

> เปล่า เขาไม่ได้สระผม เขาสระผมวันเว้นวัน
>
> No, she didn't. She washes her hair every other day.

เขาไปโรงเรียนหรือเปล่า

Did she go to school?

> เปล่า เขาไม่ได้ไปโรงเรียน
>
> No, she didn't go to school.

เขาอาบน้ำแล้วหรือยัง

Has he already had a bath?

124

อาบแล้ว
He has had a bath already.
ยังไม่ได้อาบ
He has not yet had a bath.

เขาทานข้าวก่อนมาโรงเรียน
She ate before going to school.

ทานข้าวเสร็จแล้ว เขาก็ไปโรงเรียน
Having finished eating, she went to school.

เขาไปโรงเรียน หลังทานข้าว
She went to school after eating.

เขาอาบน้ำ กินข้าว แล้วเขาก็ไปโรงเรียน
She had a bath, ate, and then she went to school.

เขาดูทีวี แปรงฟัน แล้วก็เข้านอน
He watched TV, brushed his teeth, and then went to bed.

ทำการบ้านเสร็จแล้ว เขาก็เข้านอน
He went to bed after finishing his homework.

เขาแต่งตัวเสร็จแล้วหรือยัง
Has he finished getting dressed?
เสร็จแล้ว
Yes, he has.
ยังไม่เสร็จ
No, not yet.

เขาไปโรงเรียนแล้วหรือยัง
Has he left for school already?
ไปแล้ว
Yes, he has.
ยังไม่ได้ไป
No, not yet.

เด็กๆ ควรกินข้าวก่อนไปโรงเรียน

Children should eat before going to school.

นักเรียนควรทำการบ้านให้เสร็จทุกวัน

Students should finish their homework everyday.

เขารีบไปโรงเรียน

She hurried to go to school.

GRAMMAR

1. ไม่ได้

To say that something is not finished (similar to past tense in English), use this pattern.

$$S + ไม่ได้ + VP$$

ไม่ได้ is never used with stative verb (SV) or such verbs as มี, อยากจะ, and ชอบ. Instead, simply use ไม่ + verb.

2. เสร็จ   to finish doing or to be done with something

To say, "I finished my work," or "I'm done eating," use เสร็จ in this pattern.

$$S + VP + เสร็จ (แล้ว)$$

e.g. นักเรียนทำการบ้านเสร็จแล้ว   The students are done with their homework.

พี่สาวทานข้าวเช้าเสร็จแล้ว   My older sister has finished eating breakfast.

To ask such questions as, "Have you finished it yet?" use this pattern.

Question	S + VP + เสร็จแล้วหรือยัง
Answer	Yes: (S + VP) + เสร็จแล้ว
	No: (S) + ยัง + (VP) + ไม่เสร็จ
	or (S + VP) + ยังไม่เสร็จ

e.g. นักเรียนทำการบ้านเสร็จแล้วหรือยัง   Have the students finished their homework?

(ทำการบ้าน) เสร็จแล้ว   Yes.

ยัง (ทำการบ้าน) ไม่เสร็จ   No.

(ทำการบ้าน) ยังไม่เสร็จ   No.

3. ควร, ควรจะ should

To say, "I should go to school," or "We should listen to our parents," use ควร in the pattern below.

$$S + ควร + VP$$

e.g. ฉันควรจะไปโรงเรียน   I should go to school.

เราควรฟังพ่อแม่   We should listen to our parents.

เราไม่ควรไปเที่ยว   We shouldn't go out.

4. ให้ so that

ให้ in directive sentences indicates result or manner (V so that SV).

e.g. พูดให้ดังๆ   Say it (so that it's) loud.

ทำงานให้เสร็จ   Finish your work.

DRILL

1. เขากำลังทำอะไร (is still sleeping)

    What is she doing?

2. เขาตื่นนอนแล้วใช่ไหม (yes)

    She has already gotten up, right?

3. เขาอาบน้ำเสร็จแล้วใช่ไหม (no, she is taking a bath)

    She has finished with her bath, right?

4. เขาอาบน้ำเสร็จแล้วหรือยัง (no, she is still taking a bath)

    Has she finished with her bath?

5. เขาไปทำงานแล้วหรือยัง (yes)

    Has she gone to work?

6. เขาทานอาหารเสร็จแล้วหรือยัง (no)

    Has she finished eating?

7. เขาทำการบ้านยังไม่เสร็จใช่ไหม (no)

    She is not done with her homework, right?

8. เขาทำการบ้านเสร็จแล้วไม่ใช่หรือ (yes)

    She is done with her homework, isn't she?

9. อาบน้ำเสร็จแล้วเขาทำอะไร (eat breakfast)

    What did he do after he finished bathing?

10. ก่อนกินข้าวเขาทำอะไร (take a bath)

    What did he do before eating?

11. เขาทำอะไรหลังอาบน้ำเสร็จ (eat breakfast)

    What did he do after he finished bathing?

12. เขากินข้าวก่อน หรือ อาบน้ำก่อน (take a bath)

    Did he eat first or bathe first?

13. กินข้าวเสร็จแล้วเขาทำอะไร (go to school)

    What did he do after eating?

PARTNER ACTIVITIES

I. Look at these pictures and write down what the person is doing.

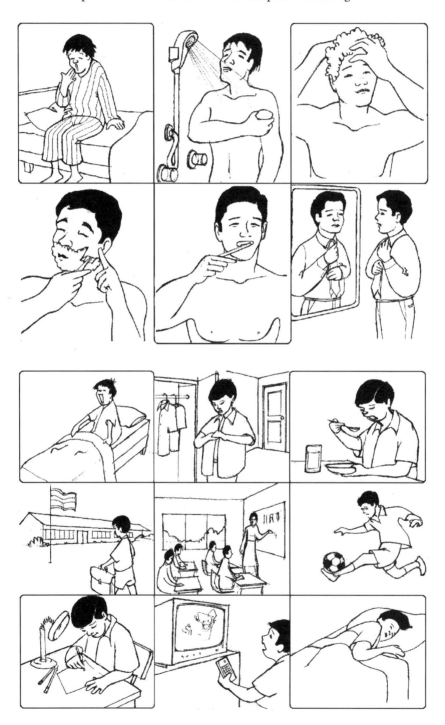

II. Based on the first set of pictures, make up statements using these words.

1. ก่อน
2. แล้วก็
3. เสร็จ
4. หลัง

III. Based on the second set of pictures, make up sentences using these words.

1. ก่อน
2. แล้วก็
3. เสร็จ
4. หลัง

IV. Ask your partner this question. ก่อนมาโรงเรียน คุณทำอะไรบ้าง Then write down the answer in the space below, using sentence connector แล้วก็.

ก่อนมาโรงเรียน   คุณ...

....

Then compare yourself with your partner, using ทั้ง......... และ......... and แต่.

1. ....
2. ....

FIND SOMEONE WHO . . .

Students circulate around the room and ask questions in the form คุณ.....ใช่ไหม. First, practice asking these questions with your teacher. Then, find two persons who . . .

1. .... bathe everyday.
2. .... shampoo everyday.
3. .... come to school everyday.
4. .... eat breakfast before coming to school.
5. .... comb their hair before getting dressed.
6. .... brush their teeth before bathing.
7. .... didn't wash their hair today.
8. .... haven't eaten yet.

CLASS ACTIVITY

Mime: Students write down an action on a piece of paper and put it in a pile. A student picks one, follows the instructions, and asks ผม/ดิฉันกำลังทำอะไร. Have the class guess the activity and write it down in Thai.

EXERCISES

I. Correcting Mistakes. Working with your partner, rewrite these sentences so that they are correct.

1. ทอมเรียนภาษาไทยมหาวิทยาลัยวอชิงตัน

....

2. เขาเป็นน่ารัก แต่เรียนเก่ง

....

3. ทอมเป็นลูกเดียว

....

4. ทอมวันนี้ต้องโรงเรียน

....

5. ก่อนตื่นนอน ทอมอาบน้ำ ไปโรงเรียน แต่งตัว แล้วก็ทานข้าว

....

6. อาบน้ำเสร็จ แล้วก็เขาไปโรงเรียน

....

II. Here are Malee's little problems. Work with your partner using ควรจะ/ไม่ควรจะ or จะต้อง/จะต้องไม่ to solve Malee's problems. Report your solutions to the class.

e.g. ถ้ามาลีหิวข้าว   เขาจะต้อง/ควรจะไปกินข้าว

ถ้ามาลีเหนื่อย   ....

ถ้ามาลีเบื่อ   ....

ถ้ามาลีไม่ค่อยสบาย   ....

ถ้ามาลีอ้วน   ....

Lesson 15: Clothing, Colors, and Shopping

🔊 **คำศัพท์**

VERBS

สวม/ใส่	to wear	เรียบร้อย	to be tidy
นุ่ง	to wear	สุภาพ	to be polite
ลอง	to try	เก่า	to be old (things)
ดู	to look at		
ลด(ราคา)	to reduce the price or to give a discount		

NOUNS

กางเกง (ตัว)	pants	รองเท้าพละ (คู่)	athletic shoes
กางเกงขาสั้น (ตัว)	shorts	รองเท้าแตะ (คู่)	sandals
กางเกงขายาว (ตัว)	long pants	รองเท้าส้นสูง (คู่)	high-heeled shoes
กางเกงยีนส์ (ตัว)	jeans	เข็มขัด (เส้น)	belt
เสื้อเชิ้ต (ตัว)	shirt	นาฬิกา (เรือน)	watch
เสื้อ (ตัว)	blouse	กระเป๋า (ใบ)	purse, bag
เสื้อแขนสั้น (ตัว)	short sleeve blouse	แว่นตา (อัน)	eyeglasses
เสื้อแขนยาว (ตัว)	long sleeve blouse	แว่นตากันแดด (อัน)	sunglasses
เสื้อยืด (ตัว)	T-shirt	แหวน (วง)	ring
กระโปรง (ตัว)	skirt	ตุ้มหู (คู่)	earrings
ชุด(กระโปรง) (ตัว)	dress	หมวก (ใบ)	hat
กางเกงใน (ตัว)	underwear	ผ้านุ่ง, ผ้าถุง, ผ้าซิ่น (ผืน)	a sarong-like lower garment worn by women
เสื้อชั้นใน (ตัว)	bra		
ถุงเท้า (คู่)	socks	ผ้าขาวม้า (ผืน)	a long strip of
ชุดว่ายน้ำ (ตัว)	swimsuit		patterned cloth worn
กางเกงว่ายน้ำ (ตัว)	swimming trunks		by men
สูท (ชุด)	suit	เบอร์	size
เครื่องแบบ (ชุด)	uniform	ขนาด (ขนาด)	size
รองเท้า (คู่)	shoes	กระเป๋าเดินทาง (ใบ)	luggage

*Words in parentheses are classifiers.

131

COLORS

สีแดง	red	สีเหลือง	yellow
สีดำ	black	สีส้ม/แสด	orange
สีขาว	white	สีชมพู	pink
สีน้ำเงิน	navy blue	สีม่วง	purple
สีฟ้า	blue	สีเทา	gray
สีเขียว	green	สีน้ำตาล	brown
สีเงิน	silver	สีทอง	gold

ADJECTIVES

สี........อ่อน	light........	e.g.	สีชมพูอ่อน	light pink
สี........แก่	dark........	e.g.	สีเขียวแก่	dark green

QUESTION WORD

เท่าไร	how much

MISC.

ไม่กี่	not many/a few
ละ	per
อื่น	other

PATTERNS

เขาใส่อะไรบ้าง

What is he wearing?

เขาใส่กางเกงขายาวสีดำ เสื้อเชิ้ตสีฟ้าอ่อน ใส่รองเท้าสีดำ และ ถุงเท้าสีขาว

He is wearing black pants, light blue shirt, black shoes, and white socks.

นักเรียนไทยต้องใส่เครื่องแบบไปโรงเรียน

Thai students have to wear uniforms to school.

ใครชอบสีแดงบ้าง

Who likes red?

เขาใส่แหวนกี่วง

How many rings is she wearing?

เขาใส่แหวนสี่วง

She is wearing four rings.

132

คุณมีกางเกงสีดำกี่ตัว

How many pairs of black pants do you have?

มีไม่กี่ตัว

Not very many/a few.

คุณเคยนุ่งผ้าถุงไหม

Have you ever worn a *phathung*?

ไม่เคยเลย

No, I have not (even once).

ผ้าขาวม้าใส่ยังไง ผมใส่ไม่เป็น

How do you wear a *pha khaoma*? I don't know how.

คนไทยชอบคนแต่งตัวสุภาพ

Thais like people who dress neatly (lit., politely).

คนนี้แต่งตัวเรียบร้อยจัง

This person dresses so neatly.

แต่งตัวให้เรียบร้อย

Dress neatly.

ขอดูเสื้อสีแดงตัวนั้นหน่อยค่ะ/ครับ

May I look at that red blouse?

ขอลองหน่อยได้ไหมคะ/ครับ

May I try it on?

ตัวนี้เล็กไป มีเบอร์ใหญ่กว่านี้ไหมคะ/ครับ

This one is too small. Do you have a bigger size?

มีสีอื่นไหมคะ/ครับ

Do you have (it) in another color?

มีสีเดียวกันอีกไหมคะ/ครับ

Do you have more in the same color?

มีตัวอื่นไหมคะ/ครับ

Do you have another one?

เสื้อตัวนี้เท่าไรคะ/ครับ แล้วตัวนั้นล่ะ

How much is this blouse? What about that one?

รองเท้าคู่ละเท่าไรคะ/ครับ

How much is a pair of shoes?

แหวนวงละเท่าไรคะ/ครับ

How much is a ring?

แพงจัง ลดหน่อยได้ไหมคะ/ครับ

It's so expensive. Could you reduce the price?

GRAMMAR

1. Classifiers

1.1. A classifier is used when one wants to quantify a noun. Use the pattern below.

Noun + Number + Classifier

e.g. เขามีเสื้อสามตัว   He has three shirts.

นักเรียนสองคนกลับบ้านแล้ว   Two students left already.

1.2. A classifier is used when one specifies a noun with a demonstrative adjective (this, that). Use this pattern.

Noun + Classifier + Demonstrative Adj.

e.g. เสื้อตัวนี้แพงมาก   This blouse is very expensive.

นาฬิกาเรือนนั้นเก่า   That watch is old.

แหวนวงไหนของคุณ   Which ring is yours?

2. เท่าไร how much

To ask for the price of something, use question word เท่าไร.

e.g. เสื้อตัวนี้(ราคา)เท่าไร   How much is this blouse?

นี่เท่าไร   How much is this?

3. ไม่กี่ not many/a few

To say, "I don't have many Thai friends," or "Few students speak Thai fluently," use
ไม่กี่ in this patterns.

S + V + DO (noun) + ไม่กี่ + Classifier
Noun + ไม่กี่ + Classifier + SV

e.g. ฉันมีเพื่อนคนไทยไม่กี่คน   I have a few Thai friends.

นักเรียนไม่กี่คนเคยไปเมืองไทย   Few students have been to Thailand.

4. ละ per

To say, "How much is a blouse?" or "A blouse is 180 baht," use ละ in the pattern
below.

Question: N + Clf + ละ + เท่าไร
Answer: N + Clf + ละ + price

e.g. หมวกใบละเท่าไร   How much is a hat?

ใบละ ๖๐ บาท   It's 60 baht.

นาฬิกาเรือนละเท่าไร   How much is a watch?

เรือนละ ๑,๒๐๐ บาท   It's 1,200 baht.

DRILL

1. คุณมีกางเกงยีนส์กี่ตัว (3)   How many jeans do you have?
2. คุณมีเสื้อยืดสีขาวกี่ตัว (5)   How many white T-shirts do you have?
3. คุณใส่แหวนกี่วง (2)   How many rings do you wear?
4. คุณมีนาฬิกากี่เรือน (1)   How many watches do you have?
5. คุณมีถุงเท้าสีขาวกี่คู่ (20)   How many white socks do you have?
6. คุณมีแว่นตากี่อัน (3)   How many eyeglasses do you have?
7. คุณมีกางเกงสีแดงกี่ตัว (none)   How many red pants do you have?
8. คุณมีผ้าถุงกี่ผืน (not many, a few)   How many *phathung* do you have?
9. คุณมีเสื้อยืดกี่ตัว (several)   How many T-shirts do you have?
10. คุณชอบสีแดงใช่ไหม (no, I like black)   You like red, don't you?

PARTNER ACTIVITIES

I. Working with a partner, write down the clothing that you see in this picture.

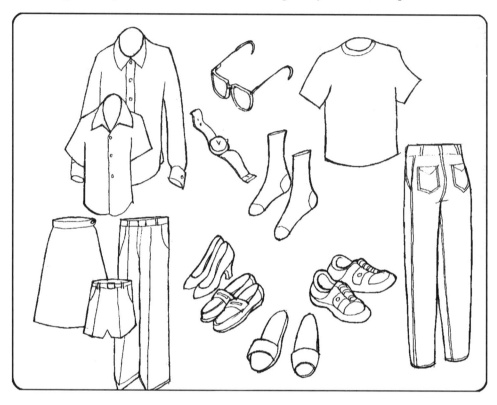

II. Teacher makes up prices and colors for the clothing in the picture. Students ask the teacher questions to find out the prices and colors of all items.

  e.g. แว่นตาอันละเท่าไร

    แว่นตาสีอะไร

III. Students take turns describing their partners' clothing.

IV. Ask your partner these questions. Then report your findings to the class.

  1. คุณมีกางเกงยีนส์กี่ตัว
  2. คุณมีเสื้อยืดสีขาวกี่ตัว
  3. คุณมีแหวนกี่วง
  4. คุณมีนาฬิกากี่เรือน
  5. คุณชอบสีอะไรบ้าง

CLASS ACTIVITIES

I. Teacher picks one student and asks the other students to describe his/her clothing.

II. Teacher briefly shows the picture of a person. Students work in groups of four, writing down what they remember about the clothing of the person in the picture. Each group reads its list to the class.

TWENTY QUESTIONS

Teacher writes down one student's name on a piece of paper. Students have to ask yes/ no questions about clothing to guess who it is.

GROUP VOCABULARY CHALLENGE

Close your book! Work in groups of four, making a list of vocabulary of clothing and colors. Which group has the most words?

EXERCISE

Correcting Classifiers: The sentences below are grammatically incorrect. Make appropriate corrections.

1. เขามีสามพี่สาว
2. คุณชอบหมวกตัวไหน
3. ถุงเท้าราคากี่เท่าไร
4. ฉันอยากซื้อเสื้อนี้
5. นาฬิกาสายนี้สวยดี
6. เขามีเพื่อนคนไทยหลาย
7. เสื้อตัว ๒๓๕ บาท
8. นักเรียนนี้เรียนภาษาไทย
9. คุณมีเสื้อยืดตัวสีขาวกี่ตัว
10. กระเป๋านี้ของใคร

CULTURAL CORNER

Unlike most Americans, Thais do "judge a book by its cover." Thais pay attentions to a person's cleanliness, neatness of appearance, and proper clothing. In some cases, appropriate clothing is absolutely required (e.g. some temples, palaces, and even some libraries). More generally, you'll find that if you dress สุภาพ or เรียบร้อย, you'll be treated especially well.

Lesson 16: Chores, Chores, Chores

 คำศัพท์

NOUNS

เงิน (บาท)	money	ห้องนอน (ห้อง)	bedroom
โต๊ะ (ตัว)	table	ห้องน้ำ (ห้อง)	bathroom
อาทิตย์ (อาทิตย์)	week	ห้องครัว (ห้อง)	kitchen
เดือน (เดือน)	month		

*Words in parentheses are classifiers.

VERBS

ทำงานบ้าน	to do housework
ทำความสะอาดบ้าน	to clean the house
กวาดบ้าน	to sweep the floor
ถูบ้าน	to mop/scrub the floor
ซักผ้า	to do laundry
ตากผ้า	to hang clothes up to dry
ทำอาหาร/ทำกับข้าว	to cook
หุงข้าว	to cook rice
ซื้อกับข้าว/จ่ายตลาด	to buy groceries
ล้างจาน	to do dishes
ปัดฝุ่น	to dust
ทิ้งขยะ	to take the garbage out
เอาขยะไปทิ้ง	to take the garbage out
เลี้ยงลูก/ดูลูก	to take care of (one's own) child
เก็บเตียง	to make the bed
ให้	to give
ยก	to lift
หนัก	to be heavy
ขอบใจ	to thank, thank you (to an inferior)

138

MISC.

ช่วย.....หน่อย	Could you please.....?
ให้	for
ไม่เป็นไร	not at all
ไหว/ไม่ไหว	can/can't (due to physical ability)
ราว	about

QUESTION WORD

บ่อยแค่ไหน	how often?

PATTERNS

เขาไม่ค่อยชอบทำงานบ้าน	He does not like to do housework that much.
ใครเป็นคนทำความสะอาดบ้าน	Who is the one who cleans the house?
แฟนเป็นคนทำ	My husband/wife does.
ใครทำอาหารให้มาลี	Who cooked for Malee?
แม่ทำอาหารให้มาลี	Her mom cooked for her.
แล้วมาลีทำอะไร	Then what did Malee do?
มาลีล้างจานให้แม่	Malee washed dishes for her mom.
ช่วยทำอาหารให้หน่อยได้ไหมคะ/ครับ	Could you please cook for me?
ได้ค่ะ/ครับ	Yes.
ไม่ได้ค่ะ/ครับ ดิฉัน/ผมไม่มีเวลา	No, I can't. I do not have time.
ช่วยซักผ้าให้หน่อยนะ	Please do the laundry for me.
ช่วยยกโต๊ะหน่อยได้ไหมคะ/ครับ	Could you please lift (move) the table?
ไม่ไหว โต๊ะตัวนี้หนักเกินไปค่ะ/ครับ	I can't. This table is too heavy.
ช่วยดูลูกให้หน่อยได้ไหม	Could you please watch my child for me?
ได้ค่ะ/ครับ	Yes.
ขอบใจมากนะ	Thank you very much.
ไม่เป็นไรค่ะ/ครับ	Not at all.
พ่อช่วยแม่ทำงานบ้าน	Dad helped Mom with the housework.

139

คุณทำความสะอาดบ้านอาทิตย์ละกี่ครั้ง	How many times a week do you clean your house?
อาทิตย์ละครั้ง	Once a week.
คุณซักผ้าบ่อยแค่ไหน	How often do you do laundry?
อาทิตย์ละ ๒-๓ ครั้ง	Two to three times a week.
คุณซื้อกับข้าว/จ่ายตลาดอาทิตย์ละกี่ครั้ง	How many times a week do you buy groceries?
ราวๆ ๓-๔ ครั้ง	About three to four times.
ช่วยทิ้งขยะให้หน่อยนะ	Please take the garbage out for me.
เอาขยะไปทิ้งด้วยนะ	Take the garbage out.
เอาขยะไปทิ้งที	Take the garbage out.
เอาขยะไปทิ้งซิ	Take the garbage out (now)!

GRAMMAR

1. ให้ for

To express, "I cooked for him," or "He cooked for me," use this pattern.

S + VP + ให้ + pronoun/noun (someone)

e.g. เขาทำความสะอาดบ้านให้ฉัน	She cleaned for me.
ฉันทำอาหารให้เขา	I cooked for her.

2. ช่วย Would you please.....?

By using the word ช่วย in the beginning of a sentence, the speaker is asking for a favor or assistance. The word หน่อย with particle นะ are often placed at the end in order to soften the request. It can also be made into a yes/no question by using ได้ไหม question tag, thus giving the chance for the listener to decline.

2.1 ช่วย + V

e.g. ช่วยทำกับข้าวหน่อยนะ	Please cook (for me).
ช่วยทำกับข้าวหน่อยได้ไหม	Could you please cook?
ช่วยล้างจานหน่อยนะ	Please do the dishes.
ช่วยพูดดังๆ หน่อย	Please speak louder.

2.2 ช่วย + **VP** + ให้ + person (first or third person)

e.g. ช่วยทำกับข้าวให้แม่หน่อยได้ไหม   Could you please cook for Mom?

ช่วยซื้อกับข้าวให้ฉันหน่อยนะ   Please buy groceries for me.

ช่วยทำความสะอาดบ้านให้ตาหน่อย   Please clean house for Grandpa.

ช่วย is also used as a regular verb which means to help or assist someone with something.

S + ช่วย + Pronoun + VP

e.g. ใครช่วยแม่ทำอาหาร   Who helped Mom cook?

เขาไม่ช่วยแม่ทำงานบ้าน   She didn't help Mom with housework.

3. ละ per

To say, "I eat three times a day," or "I bought groceries once a week," use ละ in this pattern.

S + VP + วัน/เดือน/อาทิตย์/ปี + ละ + Number + ครั้ง

e.g. เขากินข้าววันละ ๓ ครั้ง   He eats three times a day.

คุณไปเมืองไทยปีละกี่ครั้ง   How many times a year do you go to Thailand?

ปีละครั้ง   Once a year.

4. Degrees of insistence when giving commands

As in extending an invitation (lesson 13), one also has a choice to be or not to be insistent as well as to vary the degree of insistence. The following patterns represent the degrees of insistence in an ascending order.

e.g. ช่วยล้างจานให้หน่อยได้ไหม

ล้างจานด้วยนะ

ช่วยล้างจานที

ล้างจานซิ

5. ไหว/ไม่ไหว can/can't

To say, "I can do this because I'm physically up to it," use ไหว instead of เป็น.

S + VP + ไหว

For the negative, use this pattern.

S + VP + ไม่ไหว

e.g. เขาเดินไหว   She can walk (has strength to walk).

เขาไปโรงเรียนไม่ไหวเพราะเขาไม่สบาย   He can't go to school because he is sick.

ฉันกินไม่ไหว อาหารมากไป   I can't eat. There is too much food.

For questions, use **ไหวไหม**   tag question.

e.g. เดินไหวไหม   Can you walk?

To answer yes: ไหว, no: ไม่ไหว.

DRILL 1

1. ใครซื้อกับข้าว (Tom)   Who bought groceries?

2. ทอมทำอะไร (cleaning the house)   What is Tom doing?

3. ทอมทำกับข้าวให้ใคร (dad)   Who did Tom cook for?

4. ใครทำกับข้าวให้พ่อ (Tom)   Who cooked for dad?

5. ใครซักผ้าให้ฉัน (mom)   Who washed clothes for me?

6. แม่ซักผ้าให้ใคร (me)   Who did mom wash clothes for?

DRILL 2

1. ช่วยทำอาหารให้หน่อยได้ไหม (yes)

2. ช่วยซื้อกับข้าวให้หน่อยได้ไหม (no, I have no money)

3. ช่วยทำกับข้าวให้หน่อยได้ไหม (no, I do not know how)

4. ช่วยดูลูกให้หน่อยได้ไหม (no, I don't have time)

5. ช่วยล้างจานให้หน่อยได้ไหม (no, I have to go to school)

6. ช่วยทำความสะอาดบ้านให้หน่อยได้ไหม (no, I don't feel well)

SUBSTITUTION DRILL

เขา	ไปซื้อของ	ได้
	เต้นรำ	
		ไม่เป็น
ฉัน		
	เล่นกีตาร์	
		ไม่ได้
	ไปเที่ยว	
พี่สาว		
	พูดภาษาไทย	
น้า		
	ไปซื้อของ	
		ไม่ไหว

PARTNER ACTIVITIES

I. Look at these pictures and decide what the person is doing.

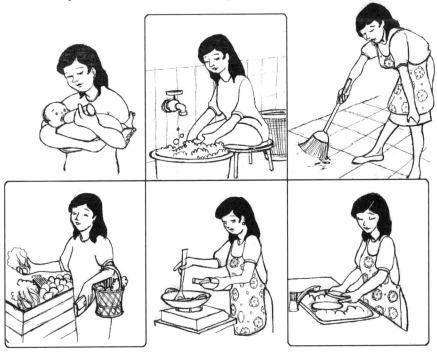

II. Write sentences based on the pictures above, using these words.

1. แล้วก็
2. ก่อน
3. หลัง

CLASS ACTIVITY

Mime: Students write down a chore on a piece of paper and put it in a pile. A student picks one, pantomimes the action, and asks **ผม/ดิฉันกำลังทำอะไร**. The class guesses the activity.

FIND SOMEONE WHO . . .

Students circulate around the classroom, asking classmates questions to find two persons who . . .

1. .... like to wash dishes.
2. .... cook everyday.
3. .... do not know how to cook.

4. .... do laundry once a week.

5. .... eat more than three times a day.

6. .... buy groceries everyday.

7. .... like to clean bathrooms.

EXERCISES

I. Read the following story, then complete your own story using the pictures on page 143.

ตามปกติ หลังตื่นนอน *มานี* มักจะหุงข้าวและทำอาหารให้ลูกๆ และสามี สามีมานี ชื่อ*มานะ* เขาทำงานที่บริษัทขายเสื้อผ้า เขาต้องไปทำงานเช้ามากทุกวัน เลยไม่มีเวลาช่วย*มานี*ทำงานบ้าน

พวกเขามีลูกด้วยกัน ๒ คน ชื่อ *เม่น* กับ *หมอก* *เม่น*อายุ ๖ ขวบ *หมอก*อายุ ๑ ขวบ *เม่น*ไปโรงเรียนแล้ว แต่*หมอก*ยังอยู่บ้านกับแม่และยาย

ตอนบ่าย...

....

ตอนเย็น...

....

(ตอนบ่าย – in the afternoon; ตอนเย็น – in the evening)

*Words in italics are names.

II. Make up questions based on the story and answer them.

1. ....

....

2. ....

....

3. ....

....

4. ....

....

5. ....

....

6. ....

....

7. ....

....

Unit 4
Time

Lesson 17: Time of Day

 คำศัพท์

TIME PHRASES

ตอนเช้ามืด	at dawn	ตอนเย็น	in the evening
ตอนเช้า	in the morning	ตอนค่ำ	early evening
ตอนสาย	in late morning	ตอนดึก	in the late night
ตอนเที่ยง	at noon	ตอนกลางวัน	in daytime
ตอนบ่าย	in early afternoon	ตอนกลางคืน	in the nightime

QUESTION WORDS

ตอนไหน	when, referring specifically to time of day
เมื่อไร, เมื่อไหร่	when

MISC.

โดยมาก	most of the time
ส่วนมาก	most, most of the time
ตอน	period

PATTERNS

ส่วนมาก คุณไปโรงเรียนตอนไหน	When do you tend to go to school?
ทำการบ้าน	do homework?
ดูทีวี	watch TV?
ออกกำลังกาย	exercise?
ดิฉัน/ผมมักจะไปโรงเรียนตอนสาย	I tend to go to school in the late morning.
ทำการบ้านตอนเย็น	I tend to do homework in the evening.
ดูทีวีตอนค่ำ	I tend to watch TV in the evening.
ออกกำลังกายตอนเช้า	I tend to exercise in the morning.

ตามปกติ คุณอาบน้ำตอนไหน ตอนเช้า หรือ ตอนค่ำ

When do you normally take a bath, in the morning or at night?

โดยมาก ผม/ดิฉันมักจะอาบน้ำตอนเช้าก่อนไปโรงเรียน

Most of the time, I bathe in the morning before going to school.

ตามปกติคุณทำอะไรบ้างตอนเย็น

What do you normally do in the evening?

ตามปกติ ตอนเย็น ดิฉัน/ผมมักจะทำกับข้าว กินข้าว ล้างจาน แล้วก็ ดูทีวี

Normally I tend to cook, eat, do dishes, and then watch TV.

เขาไปซื้อของเมื่อไร

When did she go shopping?

ตอนเช้า

In the morning.

นักเรียนส่วนมากไปโรงเรียนตอนเช้า

Most students go to school in the morning.

GRAMMAR

1. โดยมาก, ส่วนมาก most of the time

Similarly to **ตามปกติ** which means normally, ordinarily, or as usual, **โดยมาก, ส่วนมาก** are placed at the beginning of a sentence.

e.g. โดยมาก คุณมักจะทำอะไรตอนเย็น

What are you likely to do in the evening most of the time?

ส่วนมาก ผมมักจะดูทีวี

I mostly watch TV.

2. ส่วนมาก most

To say, "Most students have been to Thailand," or "Most Americans like Thai food," use **ส่วนมาก** in the pattern below.

S + ส่วนมาก + VP

e.g. นักเรียนส่วนมากเคยไปเมืองไทย

คนอเมริกันส่วนมากชอบอาหารไทย

3. ตอนไหน when (what time of day)

To find out at what time of day someone does something, use **ตอนไหน** as a question word. ตอนไหน literally means "which period."

e.g. เขาเข้านอนตอนไหน   When did she go to bed?

      ตอนค่ำ   (She went to bed) early evening.

      ตอนดึก   (She went to bed) late at night.

 DRILL

1. เขาอาบน้ำตอนไหน (in the morning)
   When did he bathe?

2. เขาไปดูหนังกับใคร (friends)
   With whom did he go to see a movie?

3. เขาดูทีวีตอนไหน (in the early evening)
   When did he watch TV?

4. ตอนบ่ายเขาทำอะไร (go to see a movie)
   What did he do in the afternoon?

5. เขาทานอาหารกลางวันเมื่อไร (at noon)
   When did he have lunch?

6. ตอนดึกเขาทำอะไร (listening to music)
   What did he do late at night?

7. เขาโทรศัพท์มาหาคุณตอนไหน (at dawn)
   When did he call you?

8. เขาทำการบ้านตอนไหน (in the afternoon)
   When did he do his homework?

(((•))) SUBSTITUTION DRILL

เด็กๆ	มักจะ	ไปโรงเรียน เล่นกีฬา	ตอนเช้า
			ตอนบ่าย
	ชอบ		
น้องชาย			
	ไม่เคย		
		ดูทีวี	
	อยาก		
อาจารย์	ไม่ค่อย		
		ไปดูหนัง	
			ตอนดึก
พ่อแม่			

PARTNER ACTIVITY

Write down what you do during particular times of the day.

	คุณ	เพื่อน
ตอนเช้า	....	....
	....	....
ตอนบ่าย	....	....
	....	....
ตอนเย็น	....	....
	....	....
ตอนค่ำ	....	....
	....	....

Ask your partner these questions, then write the answers in the spaces provided above.

1. คุณทำอะไรบ้างตอนเช้า
2. คุณทำอะไรบ้างตอนบ่าย
3. คุณทำอะไรบ้างตอนเย็น
4. คุณทำอะไรบ้างตอนค่ำ

Compare your day with your partner. What is the same (เหมือนกัน)? What is different (ต่างกัน)? Tell the class.

PARTNER INTERVIEW

Find a different partner and ask these questions. Write down the answers, then report to the class.

1. คุณอาบน้ำตอนไหน
2. คุณทำการบ้านตอนไหน
3. คุณดูทีวีตอนไหน
4. คุณออกกำลังกายตอนไหน

CLASS ACTIVITY

Ask the teacher when this person does these activities.

เขา.................ตอนไหน

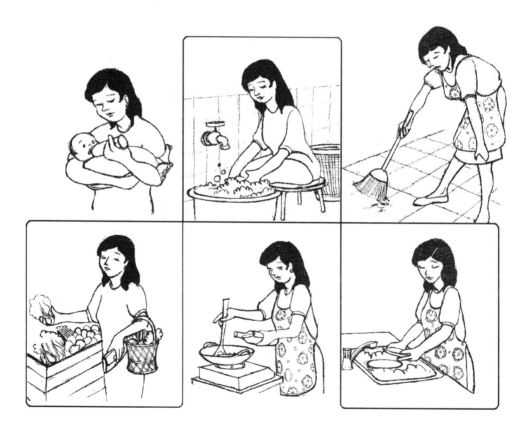

WRITING EXERCISE

Write five sentences (in Thai) based on the information above.

1. ....

2. ....

3. ....

4. ....

5. ....

Lesson 18: Colloquial Thai Time

 คำศัพท์

VERBS

ตรงเวลา	to be on time	เปิด	to open
ทันเวลา	to be in time	ปิด	to close
เริ่ม	to begin	ช้า, สาย	to be late
เลิก	to be over	เร็ว	to be early, fast
		ไปถึง/มาถึง	to arrive

NOUNS

นาฬิกา	o'clock (formal)	นาที (นาที)	minute
ชั่วโมง(ชั่วโมง)	hour	วินาที (วินาที)	second

*Words in parentheses are classifiers.

MISC.

ตรง	exactly, sharp
ครึ่ง	half
อีก	another
ประมาณ	about
โมง	o'clock (colloq.)
ตั้งแต่.....จนถึง	from.....until
.....โมงเช้า	o'clock in the morning (6 a.m.–11 a.m.)
เที่ยง (วัน)	noon
บ่าย.....โมง	o'clock in the afternoon (1 p.m.–3 p.m.)
.....โมงเย็น	o'clock in late afternoon (4 p.m.–6 p.m.)
.....ทุ่ม	o'clock at night (7 p.m.–11 p.m.)
เที่ยงคืน/สองยาม	midnight
ตี.....	o'clock in the early morning (1 a.m.–5 a.m.)
เสมอ	always
เวลา	at

QUESTION WORDS

กี่โมง   What time is it? (how many hours?)

COLLOQUIAL THAI TIME

A.M.

ตีหนึ่ง	one in the morning
ตีสอง	two in the morning
ตีสาม	three in the morning
ตีสี่	four in the morning
ตีห้า	five in the morning
หกโมงเช้า	six o'clock in the morning
เจ็ดโมงเช้า/(หนึ่ง)โมงเช้า	seven o'clock in the morning
แปดโมงเช้า/สองโมงเช้า	eight o'clock in the morning
เก้าโมงเช้า/สามโมงเช้า	nine o'clock in the morning
สิบโมงเช้า/สี่โมงเช้า	ten o'clock in the morning
สิบเอ็ดโมงเช้า/ห้าโมงเช้า	eleven o'clock in the morning

P.M.

เที่ยง	noon
บ่าย(หนึ่ง)โมง	one o'clock in the afternoon
บ่ายสองโมง	two o'clock in the afternoon
บ่ายสามโมง	three o'clock in the afternoon
บ่ายสี่โมง/สี่โมงเย็น	four o'clock in the afternoon
ห้าโมงเย็น	five o'clock in the evening
หกโมงเย็น	six o'clock in the evening
หนึ่งทุ่ม	seven o'clock at night
สองทุ่ม	eight o'clock at night
สามทุ่ม	nine o'clock at night
สี่ทุ่ม	ten o'clock at night
ห้าทุ่ม	eleven o'clock at night
เที่ยงคืน	midnight

PATTERNS

ตอนนี้กี่โมงแล้ว	What time is it now?
บ่ายโมงตรง	One o'clock (in the afternoon) sharp.
๕ โมง ๑๐ นาที	Five ten.
๖ โมงครึ่ง	Six thirty.
อีก ๑๕ นาทีเที่ยง	Fifteen minutes to twelve (in another fifteen minutes it will be noon).
ตามปกติคุณทานข้าวเช้ากี่โมง	Normally what time do you eat breakfast?
ราวๆ ๒ โมงเช้า	Around eight o'clock in the morning.
คุณเข้านอนกี่ทุ่ม	What time do you go to bed?
ห้าทุ่มครึ่ง	Eleven thirty.
เขามาโรงเรียนตรงเวลาไหม	Did he come to school on time?
เขามาตรงเวลา	Yes, he did.
เขามาช้าเสมอ	He is always late.
เขามาช้าบ่อยๆ แต่วันนี้เขามาเร็ว	He is often late but he is early today.
เรามาถึงโรงเรียนเวลาเดียวกัน	We arrived at school at the same time.
ร้านอาหารเปิดกี่โมง/เมื่อไร	What time does the restaurant open?
เปิด ๔ โมงเช้า	(It) opens at ten in the morning.
แล้วปิดกี่โมง	What about closing time?
ปิด ๓ ทุ่ม	(It) closes at nine at night.
ร้านอาหารเปิดเวลา ๑๐ นาฬิกา	The restaurant opens at ten o'clock in the morning and
แล้วปิดเวลา ๒๑ นาฬิกา	closes at nine o'clock at night.
เขาไปถึงโรงหนังทันเวลาไหม	Did she get to the theater in time?
เขาไปทัน(เวลา)	Yes, she arrived in time.
เขาไปไม่ทัน(เวลา)	No, she didn't arrive in time. (She missed the movie.)
เขาทำงานตั้งแต่กี่โมงถึงกี่โมง	When does she work (from what time to what time)?
ตั้งแต่ สามโมงเช้า ถึงห้าโมงเย็น	From nine in the morning until five in the evening.

154

คุณเริ่มเรียนภาษาไทยกี่โมง

    เริ่มเรียนเวลาเที่ยงครึ่ง

What time do you start studying Thai?

    Half past twelve.

คุณเลิกเรียน/เรียนเสร็จกี่โมง

    เลิกเรียน/เรียนเสร็จเวลาบ่ายโมงครึ่ง

What time do you finish studying Thai?

    One thirty (in the afternoon).

GRAMMAR

1. เสมอ always

To say, "They always eat before going to school," or "I always get up before nine," use เสมอ as in this pattern.

> S + VP + เสมอ

e.g. ฉันทานข้าวเช้าก่อนไปโรงเรียนเสมอ

    I always eat before going to school.

    เขาเข้านอนก่อนเที่ยงคืนเสมอ

    He always goes to bed before midnight.

    พ่ออ่านหนังสือก่อนนอนเสมอ

    Dad always reads before going to bed.

Note: เสมอ does not have a negative form.

2. เวลา at

To say, "I woke up at seven o'clock," เวลา is used as preposition "at." It is often omitted in spoken language.

e.g. ร้านเปิดเวลาห้าโมงเช้า   The store is open at eleven in the morning.

    เขากลับบ้านเวลาห้าโมงเย็น   She went home at five in the evening.

DRILL

  1. ตามปกติคุณตื่นนอนกี่โมง (six in the morning)

      What time do you get up normally?

  2. คุณไปโรงเรียนกี่โมง (eight in the morning)

      What time do you go to school?

  3. คุณทานข้าวเช้ากี่โมง (seven in the morning)

      What time do you eat breakfast?

  4. คุณทานข้าวกลางวันกี่โมง (noon)

      What time do you eat lunch?

5. คุณเรียนตั้งแต่กี่โมงจนถึงกี่โมง (from nine to noon)

   You study from what time to what time?

6. คุณกลับบ้านกี่โมง   (three in the afternoon)

   What time do you go home?

7. คุณทานข้าวเย็นกี่โมง (seven at night)

   What time do you eat dinner?

8. แล้วคุณจะเข้านอนกี่โมง (eleven at night)

   What time do you go to bed?

PARTNER ACTIVITIES

I. Working with a partner, fill in the clocks with colloquial Thai time.

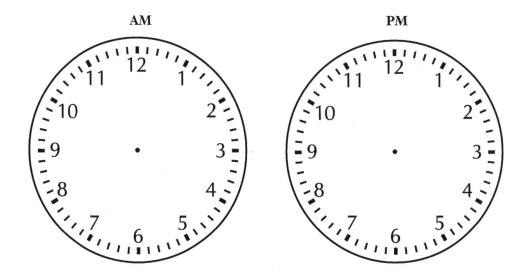

AM   **PM**

II. Interview your partner and then report to the class, using the paragraph provided.

1. คุณตื่นนอนกี่โมง

2. คุณทานอาหารเช้ากี่โมง

3. คุณมาถึงโรงเรียนกี่โมง

4. คุณทานอาหารกลางวันกี่โมง

5. คุณเรียนตั้งแต่กี่โมงจนถึงกี่โมง

6. คุณกลับบ้านกี่โมง

7. คุณทานข้าวเย็นกี่โมง

คุณ......(name)......ตื่นนอนเวลา..............แล้วก็ทานอาหารเช้าเวลา..............อาหารกลางวัน
เวลา..............และอาหารเย็นเวลา..............เขาอยู่ที่โรงเรียนตั้งแต่...........จนถึง...........และเขา
กลับบ้านเวลา...............

FIND SOMEONE WHO . . .

Students circulate around the room asking classmates questions to find two persons
who . . .

1................ get up before 7 a.m.

2................ come to school everyday.

3................ eat lunch before noon.

4................ do not eat breakfast.

5................ go to bed after midnight.

CLASS ACTIVITY

Listening Comprehension: Students find out from the teacher when/at what time the
boy was doing these activities.

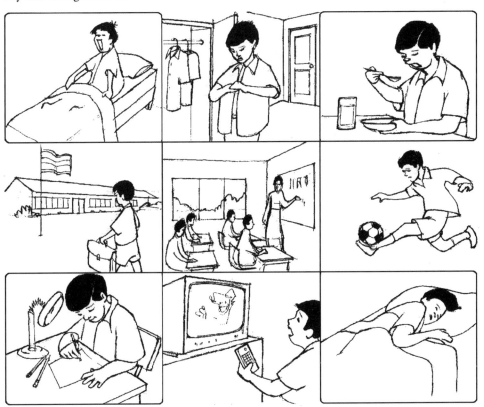

EXERCISE

Fill in the blanks with these words.

โมง   ทุ่ม   บ่าย   ดึก   โมงเช้า   เที่ยง   เย็น   ตี   โมงเย็น   เช้า

สมชาย: ....นี้เธอว่างไหม ไปดูหนังกันมั้ย

สุดา: จะไปกี่.................ล่ะ

สมชาย: เจอกันหนึ่ง................. ดีไหม ไปกินข้าวก่อนแล้วค่อยไปดูหนัง

สุดา: ไปกินข้าวห้า.................ดีกว่า แล้วไปดูหนังราวๆ หนึ่งทุ่ม
ฉันไม่อยากกลับบ้าน.................

สมชาย: ฉันก็เหมือนกัน เมื่อคืนนี้ฉันกลับบ้าน.................สอง พ่อกับแม่บ่นใหญ่เลย

สุดา: พรุ่งนี้เธอเรียนหนังสือกี่โมง

สมชาย: ตั้งแต่ ห้า.................ถึง.................สามโมง แล้วเธอล่ะ

สุดา: ฉันมีเรียนตั้งแต่โมง.................จนถึง.................

CULTURAL CORNER

In Thailand, the 24-hour clock, or military time, is officially used (e.g. 16:00 o'clock is 16 น. หรือ 16 นาฬิกา), but colloquial Thai time is used in everyday life, which can be confusing to language learners. Two o'clock could mean both eight in the morning, or two in the afternoon! It is helpful to familiarize yourself with the Thai system.

First, it is important to notice that a day is divided into four blocks of time. The four blocks are:

1. ตี (early morning from 1 a.m. to 5 a.m.)
2. เช้า (morning from 6 a.m. to 11 a.m.)
3. บ่าย/เย็น (afternoon to early evening from 1 p.m. to 6 p.m.)
4. ทุ่ม (late evening from 7 p.m. to 11 p.m.)

Second, 12:00 and 7:00 begin the blocks.

In the morning, 7 a.m. is called หนึ่งโมงเช้า and 7 p.m. is called หนึ่งทุ่ม.

In this respect, 8 a.m. can be called สองโมงเช้า and 9 a.m. สามโมงเช้า. The same is true with 8 p.m. and 9 p.m. which are สองทุ่ม and สามทุ่ม respectively.

If the context is not clear, one needs to specify the time of when making an appointment. I have witnessed this type of mishap during one of our conferences onThai language. Two persons were planning to have a meal together at five. One showed up at 11:00 a.m., while the other showed up at 5:00 p.m. And they were both professors of Thai!

Lesson 19: Time Words—
Past, Present, and Future

PAST		PRESENT		FUTURE	
เมื่อเช้านี้	this morning	วันนี้	today	พรุ่งนี้	tomorrow
เมื่อคืนนี้	last night	เดี๋ยวนี้	now	คืนนี้	tonight
เมื่อเร็วๆ นี้	recently			เดี๋ยว	just a moment
เมื่อกี้นี้	a moment ago			มะรืนนี้	the day after
เมื่อวานนี้	yesterday				tomorrow
เมื่อวานซืน	the day before			เร็วๆ นี้	soon
	yesterday				
วันก่อน	the other day			วันหน้า	some day (in future)
เมื่อก่อน	previously			วันหลัง	some day (in future)
อาทิตย์ก่อน/ที่แล้ว	last week/	อาทิตย์นี้	this week	อาทิตย์หน้า	next week
	...week(s) ago				
สัปดาห์ก่อน/ที่แล้ว	last week/	สัปดาห์นี้	this week	สัปดาห์หน้า	next week
	...week(s) ago				
เดือนก่อน/ที่แล้ว	last month/	เดือนนี้	this month	เดือนหน้า	next month
	...month(s) ago				
ปีก่อน/ที่แล้ว	last year/	ปีนี้	this year	ปีหน้า	next year
	...year(s) ago				

PRE-VERB

จะ   will (future tense marker)

VERBS

แน่   to be certain, to be sure

จบ   to finish to the end, to complete

MISC.

บาง   every

ถ้าไม่.....ก็   if not.....then.....

PATTERNS

เมื่อวานนี้ คุณไปทำงานหรือเปล่า	Did you go to work yesterday or not?
ไปค่ะ/ครับ	Yes, I did.
ไม่ได้ไปค่ะ/ครับ	No, I didn't.
เมื่อกี้นี้ คุณไปไหนมา	Where did you just go?
ไปหาอาจารย์มา	I went to see my professor.
ไปกินข้าวมา	I went to eat.
เมื่อคืนนี้คุณทำอะไรบ้าง	What did you do last night?
ไปดูหนังมา	I went to see a movie.
ไปเที่ยวบ้านเพื่อนมา	I went to a friend's house.
คุณพบกับเขาเมื่อไร	When did you meet her?
เมื่อเร็วๆนี้	Recently.
เมื่อกี้นี้	Just a moment ago.
เมื่อวันก่อน	The other day.
คุณจะพบเขาอีกเมื่อไร	When will you meet her again?
เร็วๆ นี้	Soon.
พรุ่งนี้	Tomorrow.
เมื่อเช้านี้ คุณไปไหนมา	Where did you go this morning?
ไปธนาคารมา	I went to the bank.
คุณเรียนภาษาไทยวันละกี่ชั่วโมง	How many hours a day do you study Thai?
วันละ ๓ ชั่วโมง	Three hours a day.
คุณไปเมืองไทยปีละกี่ครั้ง	How many times a year do you go to Thailand?
ปีละครั้ง ตามปกติดิฉัน/ผมไป	Once a year. I usually go to Thailand every
เมืองไทยทุกปี แต่บางปีก็ไม่ได้ไป	year. But some years, I don't go.
เมื่อก่อนนี้ เขาเคยอยู่ที่เมืองไทย	He used to live in Thailand, but he lives in
แต่เดี๋ยวนี้ เขาอยู่ที่ซีแอตเติล	Seattle now.

160

ปีหน้าคุณจะไปเมืองไทยมั้ย	Will you go to Thailand next year?
ปีหน้า คุณจะเรียนอะไร	What will you study next year?
ยังไม่แน่ ถ้าไม่เรียนภาษาไทย	(I'm) not sure. If I don't study Thai, I'll study
ก็จะเรียนภาษาจีน	Chinese.
คุณจะไปเมืองไทยเมื่อไร	When will you go to Thailand?
อีกสองปี	In two years.
(ถ้า)ไม่ปีนี้ก็ปีหน้า	If not this year then next year.
คุณจะไปไหน	Where are you going?
(ถ้า)ไม่ไปดูหนังก็จะไปซื้อของ	If I don't go see a movie, then I'll go shopping.
คุณจะอยู่ที่นี่อีกนานเท่าไร	How much longer will you be here?
อีกหนึ่งเดือน	Another month.
เขาไปเมืองไทยสองปีก่อน	He went to Thailand two years ago.
นักเรียนบางคนเคยไปเมืองไทย	Some students have been to Thailand.
เขาจะเรียนจบปีหน้า	She will graduate next year.
เขาอ่านหนังสือจบแล้ว	He finished the book.
หนังจบแล้ว	The movie is over.

GRAMMAR

1. จะ shall, will

To say, "I will meet him tomorrow," or "He will see me," use **จะ** in front of the verb.

> จะ + Verb

e.g. (เดี๋ยว)คุณจะไปไหน	Where are you going?
จะกลับบ้าน	I'm going home.
จะไปธุระ	I'm going to run an errand.
จะไปทานข้าว	I'm going to eat.

161

2. มา

มา is a secondary verb used with ไป, corresponding to present perfect tense in English.

e.g.	เมื่อกี้นี้ คุณไปไหนมา	Where did you just go?
	ไปซื้อของมา	I went shopping.
	ไปเดินเล่นมา	I went out for a walk.
	ไม่ได้ไปไหน	I didn't go anywhere.

3. (ถ้า)ไม่.....ก็ If not.....then

To say, "If it's not this restaurant, it's that one," or "If it's not you, then it's me," (i.e. you are not sure which one), use this pattern.

ถ้าไม่ + VP + ก็ + VP

e.g.	ถ้าไม่ไปวันนี้ ก็จะไปพรุ่งนี้	If (I) don't go today, then I'll go tomorrow.
	ถ้าไม่อยู่ที่นี่ ก็อยู่ที่นั่น	If it's not here, then it's there.
	ถ้าไม่ใช่คนนี้ก็คนนั้น	If it's not this person, then it's that person.

4. Pre-numerals ทุก (every), บาง (some)

Like **หลาย**, **ทุก** and **บาง** are pre-numerals and thus must be accompanied by classifiers, as in the pattern below.

Noun + หลาย / ทุก / บาง + Classifier

e.g.	อาหารทุกอย่างไม่อร่อย	Every dish is not delicious.
	อาหารบางอย่างไม่อร่อย	Some dishes are not delicious.
	เด็กทุกคนเป็นเด็กดี	Every child is a good child.
	นักเรียนหลายคนไม่สบาย	Several students are sick.
	เขามีลูกหลายคน	She has several children.
	เขาพูดได้หลายภาษา	She can speak several languages.

FIND SOMEONE WHO . . .

Students circulate around the room asking classmates questions to find someone who . . .

.... will go to see a movie tonight.

.... will stay home this evening.

.... will go out with his/her แฟน tomorrow.

.... will go to Thailand this year.

.... ate out last night.

...............went to Thailand last year.

CLASS ACTIVITIES

I. Work in groups of three or four. Make a list of things you would like to do this evening. Read the list to the class.

II. Game: First, Second, Third

Ask students to arrange themselves in order of:

the time they got up this morning;

the time they went to bed last night;

the time they will go home today.

III. Find out from the teacher when these people are going to Thailand.

IV. Find out from the teacher when these people exercised.

V. Find out from the teacher how many times this woman does these activities in a day or a week.

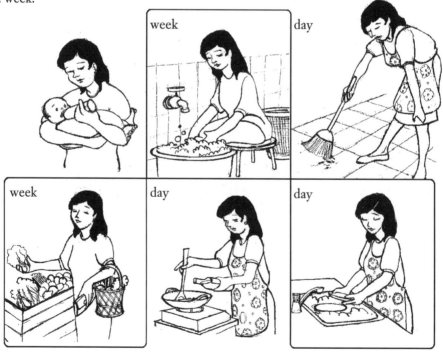

EXERCISE

Translate these sentences into Thai.

1. He should go to Thailand this year.

2. Students must not talk in class. ("Every student must not talk in class.")

3. What did you do last night?

4. I have to go visit my parents next week.

5. This morning he woke up at six o'clock.

6. I just finished my homework a moment ago.

7. Will you go to school tomorrow?

8. Now he lives in Seattle.

9. I met him at a hospital recently.

10. I went grocery shopping yesterday.

CULTURAL CORNER

จะไปไหน or ไปไหนมา sometimes are used as greetings among acquaintances. They are used to initiate conversation, not really to find out where you are going or where you have been. Sometimes Thai people will greet their friends with กิน (ทาน) ข้าวแล้วหรือยัง? (Have you eaten?).

Lesson 20: Days of the Week, Months, and Seasons

 คำศัพท์

Days

วันอาทิตย์	Sunday	วันธรรมดา	weekdays
วันจันทร์	Monday	วันเสาร์อาทิตย์	weekend
วันอังคาร	Tuesday	วันสุดสัปดาห์	weekend
วันพุธ	Wednesday	วันหยุด	holiday
วันพฤหัส(บดี)	Thursday		
วันศุกร์	Friday		
วันเสาร์	Saturday		

Months

มกราคม (ม.ค.)	January	กรกฎาคม (ก.ค.)	July
กุมภาพันธ์ (ก.พ.)	February	สิงหาคม (ส.ค.)	August
มีนาคม (มี.ค.)	March	กันยายน (ก.ย.)	September
เมษายน (เม.ย.)	April	ตุลาคม (ต.ค.)	October
พฤษภาคม (พ.ค.)	May	พฤศจิกายน (พ.ย.)	November
มิถุนายน (มิ.ย.)	June	ธันวาคม (ธ.ค.)	December

Seasons

หน้า/ฤดู	season
หน้า/ฤดูร้อน	summer
หน้า/ฤดูฝน	rainy season
หน้า/ฤดูหนาว	winter
ฤดูใบไม้ร่วง	fall or autumn
ฤดูใบไม้ผลิ	spring

NOUNS

อากาศ	weather
ฝน	rain
หิมะ	snow
พายุ	storm
มรสุม	monsoon
ปฏิทิน	calendar

VERBS

ตก	to fall
อบอ้าว	to be hot and humid
เกิด	to be born

CONJUNCTIONS

พอ.....ก็	as soon as
เวลา	when
ตอน	(during the period) when

PATTERNS

วันนี้วันอะไร	What day is it today?
วันนี้วันจันทร์	Today is Monday.
วันนี้วันที่เท่าไร	What is today's date?
วันนี้วันจันทร์ที่ ๑๖ เมษายน	Today is Monday, April 16, 2007
พ.ศ. ๒๕๕๐	
คุณเกิดวันไหน	On which day were you born?
ดิฉัน/ผมเกิดวันอาทิตย์	I was born on Sunday.
คุณเกิดวันที่เท่าไร	When is your birthday?
ดิฉัน/ผมเกิดวันที่ ๒๖ เดือนมกราคม	I was born on January 26.
วันนี้วันจันทร์หรือวันอังคาร	Is today Monday or Tuesday?
วันนี้วันอังคาร ไม่ใช่วันจันทร์	Today is Tuesday, not Monday.

167

คุณจะไปเมืองไทยเดือนนี้หรือเดือนหน้า	You are going to Thailand this month or next month?
เดือนนี้	This month.
วันนี้อากาศดี ไม่ร้อนไม่หนาว(เกินไป)	Today's weather is nice—not too hot, not too cold.
ที่เมืองไทยไม่มีฤดูใบไม้ร่วง หรือ ฤดูใบไม้ผลิ	In Thailand, there is no autumn or spring.
พอฝนตก เขาก็รีบกลับบ้าน	As soon as it began to rain, he hurried home.
พอเรียนเสร็จ เขาก็ไปกินข้าว	As soon as class was over, she went to eat.
เขาชอบอยู่บ้าน เวลาฝนตก	He likes/tends to stay home when it rains.
พี่สาวชอบร้องไห้เวลากลุ้มใจ	My older sister tends to cry when she is upset.
นักเรียนไม่ควรคุยกัน เวลาอาจารย์สอน	Students shouldn't talk when the teacher is teaching.
ฝนตกทุกวันตอนเขาอยู่เมืองไทย	It rained everyday when he was in Thailand.
ไม่ค่อยมีคนไปเดินเล่นตอนฝนตก	Hardly anyone goes out for a walk when it is raining.

GRAMMAR

Temporal Phrases

1. ตอน when

1.1 **ตอน** + noun (implies a period of time, either past or present)

e.g. ตอนเช้า ตอนสาย ตอนกลางวัน etc.

1.2 **ตอน** + clause (when = during the time when)

e.g. ผมมีเพื่อนคนไทยหลายคนตอนอยู่เมืองไทย

I had many Thai friends when (I) lived in Thailand.

ตอน (ฉันเป็น) เด็ก ฉันไม่ชอบทานข้าว

When I was young, I did not like to eat.

2. เวลา when

เวลา + clause (when = timeless, or true at all times; habitual)

e.g. เวลาอาจารย์สอน อย่าคุยกัน

Do not talk when the teacher is teaching.

เวลาฉันไม่อยู่บ้าน ชอบมีคนโทรมา

People tend to call me when I'm not home.

เขาชอบร้องไห้เวลาโมโห

She tends to cry when angry.

3. พอ.....ก็ as soon as

พอ + clause + (subj.) + ก็ + VP

e.g. พอตื่นนอน เขาก็อาบน้ำ แปรงฟัน

As soon as he got up, he took a bath and brushed his teeth.

พอเห็นอาจารย์ เขาก็รีบวิ่งมาหา

As soon as she saw the professor, she hurriedly ran to her.

พอถึงเดือนมิถุนา ครอบครัวเขาก็ไปเมืองไทย

As soon as it was June, his family went to Thailand.

PARTNER INTERVIEW

Practice these questions with your teacher. Then ask your partner these questions and report to the class.

1. When is your birthday?

2. Which days do you go to school?

3. What did you do last weekend?

4. What will you do next weekend?

CLASS ACTIVITY

Working in groups of four, ask everyone in your group these questions. Keep track of how many students say yes, no, and sometimes.

	ใช่	บางครั้ง	ไม่ใช่
1. มักจะนอนตื่นสายวันอาทิตย์ใช่ไหม	....	....	....
2. มักจะไปซื้อกับข้าวบ่ายวันเสาร์ใช่ไหม	....	....	....
3. มักจะนอนดึกวันศุกร์หรือวันเสาร์ใช่ไหม	....	....	....
4. มักจะทำงานวันเสาร์อาทิตย์ใช่ไหม	....	....	....

WHAT'S THE DEAL?

ราคาต่อ ๑ ท่าน	วันนี้ - ๓๐ เม.ย. ๕๐		๑ พ.ค. - ๓๑ ต.ค. ๕๐	
	วันเสาร์อาทิตย์	วันธรรมดา	วันเสาร์อาทิตย์	วันธรรมดา
ผู้ใหญ่ (พักห้องละ ๒ ท่าน)	๒,๑๕๐	๑,๘๕๐	๑,๙๕๐	๑,๖๕๐
ห้องพักเดี่ยว จ่ายเพิ่ม	๑,๙๐๐	๑,๖๐๐	๑,๗๕๐	๑,๔๕๐
เด็ก (อายุต่ำกว่า ๑๒ ปี พักกับ ผู้ใหญ่)	๖๐๐	๖๐๐	๖๐๐	๖๐๐

Source: The Empress Hotel, Chiang Mai

This is an advertisement for a family package from a luxury hotel in Thailand. Based on the information given, answer the following questions.

1. When is this package offered (what year)?................

2. There are two sets of dates in this promotion.

   When does the first period end?.................

   When does the second period end?................

3. If you want to stay there during the first period, how much does it cost for weekdays? And how much does it cost during weekends?

   Weekdays cost .... a day.

   Weekends cost .... a day.

4. If you want to stay there during the second period, how much does it cost for weekdays? And how much does it cost during weekends?

   Weekdays cost .... a day.

   Weekends cost .... a day.

FAMILY BIRTHDAYS

Using kinship terms, find out from the teacher on which day these people were born.

คุณ

WRITING EXERCISE

Translate these sentences into Thai.

1. Previously John was very thin. Now he is very fat.

2. John got married last year. Now he is divorced.

3. I didn't eat breakfast this morning.

4. John just called me a moment ago.

5. I will meet you on the night of the fifth at eight p.m.

6. Just as soon as Mom finished cooking, we ate dinner.

7. When I was young, I did not like to take naps.

8. Your friend came calling for you when you were not home.

9. I don't like to go to the doctor when I am sick.

10. I feel sad when I talk about my ex-boyfriend.

CULTURAL CORNER

  Thai people write dates in this sequence: วันที่ then เดือน then ปี. When someone writes 12/2, it means February 12, not December 2. To convert the Western year
(A.D.) to the Thai year (Buddhist Era, B.E.), add 543 to the A.D. year. Thus A.D.
2005 is equivalent to 2548 B.E.

Unit 5
Food

Lesson 21: At The Market

(((•))) คำศัพท์

VERBS

รับ	to take	พอ	to be enough
เอา	to want (colloquial)	เชิญ	to invite/to go ahead
ซื้อ	to buy		(please)
ขาย	to sell	ชิม	to taste, try
ทอน	to give change		

NOUNS

ตลาด (แห่ง)	market	ของกิน (อย่าง)	things to eat
ซูเปอร์มาร์เก็ต (แห่ง)	supermarket	ลูกค้า (คน)	customer
ตลาดนัด (แห่ง)	flea market	เงิน, สตางค์, ตังค์ (บาท)	money
ของใช้ (อย่าง)	things to use, utensils		

ข้าว[สาร]	[uncooked] rice
ข้าวเหนียว	sticky rice
ขนมปัง	bread
แป้ง	flour

เนื้อสัตว์ (ชนิด,อย่าง)	meat	ปลาหมึก	squid
ไก่	chicken	หอย	shellfish
หมู	pork	ปู	crab
เนื้อวัว	beef	อาหารทะเล	seafood
เป็ด	duck	ไข่ไก่/ไข่เป็ด (ฟอง)	eggs (chicken/duck)
กุ้ง	shrimp	เครื่องใน	innards
ปลา	fish		

*Words in parentheses are classifiers. The classifier for a whole animal is ตัว; otherwise, the unit of sale (e.g. กก., ขีด, ชิ้น) is used.

174

ผัก (ชนิด, อย่าง)	vegetables	ผักคะน้า (ต้น)	Chinese broccoli
ผักบุ้ง (ต้น)	morning glory	มันฝรั่ง (หัว)	potato
แตงกวา (ลูก)	cucumber	เห็ด (ดอก)	mushroom
ถั่วงอก	bean sprouts	กะหล่ำปลี (หัว)	cabbage
ข้าวโพด (ฝัก)	corn	ผักกาดหอม (ต้น)	lettuce
มะเขือ (ลูก)	eggplant	หอม (หัว)	onion
มะเขือเทศ (ลูก)	tomato	หอมแดง (หัว)	shallot
พริก (เม็ด)	chili pepper	กระเทียม (หัว)	garlic
ต้นหอม (ต้น)	green onion	มะนาว (ลูก)	lime
ผักชี (ต้น)	coriander		

ผลไม้ (ชนิด, อย่าง)	fruit	มะละกอ (ลูก)	papaya
กล้วย (ลูก, หวี)	banana	สับปะรด (ผล)	pineapple
องุ่น (ลูก, พวง)	grapes	ฝรั่ง (ลูก)	guava
ส้ม (ลูก)	orange	เงาะ (ลูก)	rambutan
มะม่วง (ลูก)	mango	มังคุด (ลูก)	mangosteen
แตงโม (ลูก)	watermelon	ลำใย (ลูก, พวง)	longan
ทุเรียน (ลูก)	durian	มะพร้าว (ลูก)	coconut

น้ำปลา	fish sauce	น้ำส้มสายชู	vinegar
น้ำตาล	sugar	น้ำมัน	cooking oil
น้ำตาลปี๊บ	palm sugar	เนย	butter
เกลือ	salt	เครื่องเทศ	seasoning, spices
ซีอิ๊ว	soy sauce	พริกไทย	black pepper

ผงซักฟอก	detergent
น้ำยาล้างจาน	dishwashing liquid

ลักษณะนาม	**CLASSIFIERS**
ชนิด/อย่าง	kind, type
กิโล/โล (กก.)	kilogram
ขีด	100 grams
ลิตร	liter
โหล	dozen
ชิ้น/อัน	piece

175

ถุง	bag, classifier for food/things that come in bags
กำ	handful (as of sand), bunch (as of vegetables)
ลูก/ผล	classifier for fruits, small roundish items
ตัว	classifier for chicken/duck/fish/crab (body of animals)
หัว	classifier for heads (as of cabbages); for bulbs, tubers, and other root vegetables, e.g. potatoes, onions, etc.
ไม้	classifier for food on sticks
ห่อ (ห่อ)	package, classifier for food that comes in packages
ซอง (ซอง)	packet/envelope, classifier for food/things that come in packets
กล่อง (ใบ)	box, classifier for things that come in boxes
ขวด (ใบ)	bottle/jar, classifier for food that comes in bottles
หลอด (หลอด)	tube, classifier for food/things that come in tubes
กระป๋อง (ใบ)	can, classifier for food/things that come in cans
แถว	classifier for a loaf of bread
แผ่น	classifier for a slice of bread
ฝัก	classifier for an ear of corn or for beans
หวี	a hand of bananas
ก้อน	classifier for things that come in lumps, e.g. soap, butter, etc.
พวง	classifier for fruits and vegetables that come in bunches, e.g. grapes.

*Words in parentheses are classifiers.

MISC.

แค่...เท่านั้น	only	จ๊ะ	polite particle
เพื่อ	in order to		

PATTERNS

จะไปไหนคะ/ครับ	Where are you going?
จะไปซื้อกับข้าวที่ตลาดค่ะ/ครับ	I'm going to buy groceries at the market.
เขาไปตลาดเพื่อซื้อกับข้าว	He went to the market to buy groceries.
คุณซื้อกับข้าวบ่อยแค่ไหน	How often do you buy groceries?
ดิฉัน/ผมซื้อกับข้าวอาทิตย์ละ ๒ ครั้ง	I buy groceries two times a week.
จะรับอะไรดีคะ/ครับ	What do you want (to buy)?

แม่ค้า นี่กิโลละเท่าไร	Street vendor, how much is this per kilo?
โลละ ๙๐ บาท	It's 90 baht a kilo.
แพงไป ลดได้มั้ยจ๊ะ	That's too expensive. Can you lower the price?
เอากี่โล	How many kilos do you want?
สองกิโลเท่านั้น	I would like two kilos only.
ถ้างั้นแปดสิบบาทก็แล้วกัน	Eighty baht, then!
ตกลง	O.K.
นี่ตังค์ทอน	Here is your change.

ผลไม้ขายยังไง ขายเป็นลูกหรือขายเป็นกิโล
How do you sell fruit? By unit or by kilo?

นี่ขายยังไง	How do you sell this?
ขายเป็นขีด	I sell it by 100 grams.
ขีดละเท่าไร	How much is it for 100 grams?
ขีดละ ๒๐ บาท	20 baht for 100 grams.
เอาสามขีด	I'll take 300 grams.

ลูกละเท่าไร	How much is it per unit?
ชิ้นละเท่าไร	How much is it per piece?
ไม้ละเท่าไร	How much is it per stick?
กำละเท่าไหร่	How much is it per bunch (vegetables)?

ลูกนี้เท่าไร	How much is this one?
ชิ้นนี้เท่าไร	How much is this piece?
ไม้นี้เท่าไร	How much is this stick?

ชิมได้ไหม	Can I taste (it)?
เชิญค่ะ/ครับ	Please go ahead.

มีทั้งของกินและของใช้ขายที่ตลาด
Both food and (other) things are sold at the market.
(There are both food and (other) things sold at the market.)

GRAMMAR

1. แค่......เท่านั้น   only

To say, "I have only 10 baht," or "This book costs only 45 baht," use แค่......เท่านั้น in pattern below.

S + VP +   แค่ + Number + (เท่านั้น)

e.g. ครอบครัวเขามีแค่สามคนเท่านั้น

There are only three people in her family.

ในห้องนี้มีนักเรียนแค่ ๑๐ คนเท่านั้น

There are only ten students in this room.

2. เพื่อ   in order to

To say, "I went to Thailand to study Thai," use เพื่อ in the pattern below.

S + VP1 +   เพื่อ + VP2

e.g. เขาไปเมืองไทยเพื่อเรียนภาษาไทย

He went to Thailand to study Thai.

เขาตื่นแต่เช้าเพื่อไปโรงเรียน

She got up early to go school.

พี่ชายออกไปข้างนอกเพื่อพบกับเพื่อนๆ

My brother went out to meet his friends.

PARTNER ACTIVITIES

I. Practice asking these questions with your teacher. Then, ask your partner these questions and report to the class.

1. How often do you go to the market?

2. Where do you buy your groceries?

3. What do you buy at the market?

4. Do you like grocery shopping?

II. Write a short paragraph on your shopping habits. Use the list of questions above as a guideline.

III. With a different partner, complete the dialogue below. Then perform the role play in front of the class.

ลูกค้า: นี่กิโลละเท่าไร

แม่ค้า: ....

ลูกค้า: ....

แม่ค้า: ลดไม่ได้เลย

ลูกค้า: แล้ว...............ล่ะ กิโลละเท่าไร

แม่ค้า: ....

ลูกค้า: ....ก็แล้วกัน

แม่ค้า: ....เอากี่กิโล

ลูกค้า: ....

CLASS ACTIVITIES

I. Find out from the teacher what these people like or don't like to eat.

II. Game: What do you have in your refrigerator?

Teacher picks one student. That student quietly tells his/her friend what he/she has in the refrigerator. The information is passed along from student to student, one at a time. The last student reveals the information given to him/her. Did he/she get it all?

EXERCISES

I. Listening Comprehension

You will hear these sentences in Thai. Number the sentences in the order that you hear them.

.... How much is it for a kilo of oranges?

.... That's too expensive. Could you give me a discount?

.... How much is it all together?

.... I don't like to cook but I like to go grocery shopping.

.... How many times a week do you buy groceries?

.... Where do you buy your groceries?

.... Thai people like to buy groceries everyday.

.... How do you sell peppers?

.... How much is a bottle of fish sauce?

.... What do you tend to buy at the market?

II. Fill in the blanks.

1. ไก่ขายยังไง: ขาย...............กิโล
2. ไก่กิโลละ...............: กิโลละ ๗๕ บาท
3. เอา...............กิโล: ๒ กิโล
4. เขาซื้อผักและผลไม้หลาย...............
5. นี่แพงไป...............ได้ไหม
6. เนื้อแพง...............หมู
7. เอาอีกไหม: ไม่เอา
   ....แล้ว
8. ที่ตลาดมี...............ของกิน...............ของใช้ขาย
9. เขาไปตลาด...............ซื้อผักและผลไม้
10. ....ตลาดมีของขายหลายอย่าง
11. มีคนขายของราวๆ ๕๐...............ที่ตลาด
12. ตลาดกับซูเปอร์มาร์เก็ต ที่ไหนแพง...............

CULTURAL CORNER

Nowadays, there are supermarkets (Western-style grocery stores) in every big city in Thailand. Big department stores in Thailand, especially in Bangkok, often have grocery stores inside, offering customers the ultimate in convenience. These supermarkets are clean and orderly, and the prices are fixed. But traditional style markets, while noisy and sometimes dirty, are lively and more interesting. Also, you can bargain there!

There is another type of market called ตลาดเย็น/ตลาดค่ำ/ตลาดนัด. These normally start around four or five p.m. These markets sell not only grocery items but also ready-made food for people to buy and take home after work, as well as clothes, toys, etc. There are also many foodstalls serving food and drink for people to eat at the market. Some of the best food in the cities can be found at these markets.

Lesson 22: At The Restaurant

((•)) **คำศัพท์**

VERBS

ขอ	to ask, to request	ต้องการ	to want
เก็บ	to collect	เอา.....มา/ไป	to bring
เลี้ยง	to treat (someone)	สั่ง	to order
จอง	to reserve	เช็ค	to check
ใส่	to put	รับประทาน	to eat (polite)
แนะนำ	to recommend, to introduce	ได้	to get, to receive
หมด	to be gone	อิ่ม	to be full

COMMAND

อย่า	do not.....

PRE-VERB

เกือบ, เกือบจะ	almost	จวน, จวนจะ	almost

FLAVORS

เค็ม	to be salty	เผ็ด	to be spicy hot
หวาน	to be sweet	จืด	to be bland
เปรี้ยว	to be sour	กำลังดี	to be perfect

COOKING TERMS

ผัด	to stir fry	e.g. ข้าวผัด, ผัดกระเพราไก่
ทอด	to fry	e.g. ไก่ทอด, ปลาทอด
ต้ม	to boil	e.g. ไข่ต้ม, ข้าวต้ม
นึ่ง	to steam	e.g. ปลานึ่ง
ย่าง, ปิ้ง	to grill	e.g. หมูย่าง, ไก่ปิ้ง

แกง	to make curry or soup	e.g. แกงไก่, แกงจืด
ยำ	to make spicy salad	e.g. ยำเนื้อ, ยำวุ้นเส้น
อบ	to bake	e.g. ไก่อบ, หมูอบ

NOUNS

อาหาร (อย่าง, ชนิด)	food (in general)
กับข้าว(อย่าง)	food to be eaten with rice
กับแกล้ม (อย่าง)	food to be eaten with alcoholic drinks
ตังค์, สตางค์, เงิน (บาท)	money
ก๋วยเตี๋ยว/ก้วยเตี๋ยว (จาน, ชาม)	noodles
ก๋วยเตี๋ยวเส้นใหญ่	broad rice noodles
ก๋วยเตี๋ยวเส้นเล็ก	small rice noodles
บะหมี่	egg noodles
เส้นหมี่	thin rice noodles
ข้าว (จาน, โถ, หม้อ)	rice
น้ำจิ้ม (ถ้วย)	dipping sauce
น้ำ (แก้ว, ถ้วย, ขวด)	water
น้ำผลไม้	juice
น้ำส้ม	orange juice
น้ำมะนาว	lemonade
น้ำอัดลม	carbonated drinks
นม	milk
กาแฟ	coffee
ชา	tea
ขนม	dessert
ของหวาน	dessert
ช้อน (คัน)	spoon
ส้อม (คัน)	fork
ช้อนส้อม (คู่)	fork and spoon
มีด (เล่ม)	knife
จาน (ใบ)	plate
ถ้วย (ใบ)	cup, small bowl
หม้อ/โถ (ใบ)	pot
ไม้จิ้มฟัน (อัน)	toothpick

ตะเกียบ (คู่)	chopsticks
หลอด (หลอด, อัน)	straw
ชาม (ใบ)	bowl
แก้ว (ใบ)	glass
ผ้าเย็น (ผืน)	cloth wipe , handiwipe

*Words in parentheses are classifiers.

CLASSIFIERS

อย่าง	kind		
ชนิด	type		
ชาม	food that comes in bowls	e.g.	ก๋วยเตี๋ยว
จาน	food that comes on plates	e.g.	ข้าวผัด
ถ้วย	food/drink that comes in cups	e.g.	ซุป, กาแฟ, ชา
แก้ว	drinks that come in glasses	e.g.	กาแฟ, น้ำส้ม
หม้อ/โถ	food that comes in pots	e.g.	ข้าว
ใบ	classifier for all empty containers		
ที่	seat/order		

PATTERNS

เชิญค่ะ กี่ที่/คนคะ	Please come in. How many people are you?
รอเดี๋ยวนะคะ จองไว้หรือเปล่า	Please wait a minute. Did you make a reservation?
มีห้องแอร์ไหม	Do you have an air-conditioned room?
ขอดูเมนูหน่อย	May I look at your menu?
ที่นี่มีอะไรอร่อยบ้าง	What dishes are good here?
อร่อยทุกอย่าง	Everything is delicious.
ที่นี่มีอาหารแนะนำอะไรบ้าง	What dishes are recommended here?
จะรับอะไรดี	What would you like to eat/order?
ขอข้าวผัดไก่ ๑ จาน	May I have a plate of chicken fried rice?
ขอข้าวผัดไก่ที่นึง	May I have an order of chicken fried rice?

ต้องการจะสั่งอะไรบ้างคะ/ครับ	What do you want to order?
คุณอยากทานอะไร	What would you like to eat?
อะไรก็ได้ ตามใจคุณ	Anything will do. It's up to you.
สั่งอาหารแล้วหรือยัง	Have you ordered yet?
สั่งแล้ว แต่ยังไม่ได้	I've already ordered but haven't gotten it yet.
สั่งกี่อย่าง	How many dishes have you ordered?
สั่งสามอย่างพอมั้ย	Will three dishes be enough?
สั่งแค่สามอย่าง พอเหรอ/หรือ	You've only ordered three dishes? Will that be enough?
เอาเผ็ดมั้ย	Would you like it spicy?
เอาเผ็ดๆ	Yes, I like it spicy.
อาหารเผ็ดไปไหม	Is the food too hot?
ไม่เผ็ดไป กำลังดี	No, it's not too hot. It's perfect.
ไม่ใส่เนื้อสัตว์/อย่าใส่เนื้อสัตว์	Do not put any meat in.
ไม่ใส่ผงชูรส/อย่าใส่ผงชูรส	Do not put in MSG.
ไม่ใส่พริก/อย่าใส่พริก	Do not put chili peppers in.
สั่ง/เอาอย่างละสามจาน/ที่	Three orders for each dish.
(เรา) สั่งอาหารอย่างเดียวกัน	We ordered the same dish.
ขอโทษค่ะ/ครับ ไก่หมดแล้ว	Sorry, the chicken is all gone.
ถ้างั้น เอาหมูก็แล้วกัน	In that case, I'll take pork.
อาหารเกือบจะเสร็จแล้วหรือยัง	Is the food almost ready?
จวนจะเสร็จแล้ว	It's almost done.
จะสั่งอะไรอีกมั้ย	Would you like to order anything else?
ไม่เอา อิ่มแล้ว	No, I'm full.

ช่วยเอาน้ำจิ้มมาให้ด้วย	Please bring (me) dipping sauce.
เก็บตังค์ด้วย (food stall)	Please collect the money (said to vendor).
ทั้งหมดเท่าไร	How much is it all together?
เช็คบิล/ขอบิลด้วย (restaurant)	Check, please.
คุณไม่ต้อง ผมเลี้ยงเอง	You don't have to (pay). I'll treat you.

GRAMMAR

1. เกือบ, เกือบจะ almost

To say, "It's almost ready," or "He is close to graduating," use this pattern.

> S + เกือบ/เกือบจะ + VP

e.g.
เขาเกือบจะไปเมืองไทยแล้ว	She has almost left for Thailand.
เกือบจะถึงเวลาเข้านอนแล้ว	It's almost bed time.
เกือบจะสามทุ่มแล้ว	It's almost nine o'clock.
เขาเกือบจะร้องไห้	He almost cried.

2. จวน, จวนจะ almost

จวน and เกือบ can be used interchangeably.

e.g.
เขาจวนจะไปเมืองไทยแล้ว
จวนจะถึงเวลาเข้านอนแล้ว
จวนจะสามทุ่มแล้ว
เขาจวนจะร้องไห้

3. QW + ก็ได้

To say "anywhere," "whatever", "whoever", use **QW + ก็ได้.**

e.g.
เราจะไปไหนก็ได้	We can go anywhere (we like).
เราจะกินอะไรก็ได้	We can eat whatever we like.
เราจะพูดกับใครก็ได้	We can talk to whoever we like.

187

4. แล้วแต่ depend on, up to

To say, "It depends on my parents," or "It depends on the economy," use this pattern.

แล้วแต่ + Noun or Pronoun

e.g. แล้วแต่คุณ   It depends on you.

แล้วแต่อากาศ   It depends on the weather.

5. เอา.....มา/ไป   to bring

To say, "I bring food to school," or "I bring food for my friend," use เอา in the patterns below.

S + เอา + Object +   มา/ไป   + Place

S + เอา + Object + มาให้/ไปให้ + Someone

e.g. ฉันเอาหนังสือไปโรงเรียน   I brought books to school.

นักเรียนเอาการบ้านไปให้ครู   Students brought the teacher homework.

PARTNER ACTIVITIES

I. Practice these questions with your teacher. Then ask your partner these questions.

1. How often do you eat out?

2. What is/are your favorite Thai restaurant(s)?

3. What are your favorite Thai dishes? What do you usually order at a Thai restaurant?

4. Can you cook Thai food?

II. ROLE PLAY I: FAST FOOD RESTAURANT

You are at a fast food joint. With your partner, complete this role play. Present your role play to the class.

แคชเชียร์: สวัสดีค่ะ จะรับอะไรดีคะ

ลูกค้า: ....

แคชเชียร์: ดื่มอะไรดีคะ

ลูกค้า: ....

แคชเชียร์: เอาอะไรอีกมั้ยคะ

ลูกค้า: ....

แคชเชียร์: ทั้งหมด ๑๑๕ บาทค่ะ

ลูกค้า: ....

แคชเชียร์: นี่ตังค์ทอน ขอบคุณค่ะ

III. ROLE PLAY II: MEAL INVITATION

With a different partner, invite a friend for a meal. Make sure to include all the details (what, where, and when).

GROUP ROLE PLAY: RESTAURANT

In a group of three or four, write a role play in a restaurant. One student is a waiter/waitress and the rest are customers. Present the role play to the class.

EXERCISE

How do you say these sentences in Thai? Practice with your teacher first.

1. Can you wait a moment?
2. Let's order now.
3. Two pots of rice are enough.
4. I want it hot.
5. We did not order fried rice, did we?
6. How many (kinds of dishes) have we ordered?
7. What are there in this dish? (What do you put in this dish?)
8. Three orders of each.
9. Would you like more rice?
10. How much is it per head/person?

CULTURAL CORNER

Thais, whether rich or poor, love to share their food. It might be a meal, a snack, some fruit, a drink, or whatever they have. Once food is offered, one should take some so as not to offend or to hurt the host's feeling, or decline politely and say that you have just eaten and/or are already full (เพิ่งทานมา หรือ อิ่มแล้ว).

American-style eating where diners take some food from every dish before starting to eat is not a common practice in Thai culture. It might be considered hoarding the food and is seen as rude. One should just take a tablespoon of one dish. Once one finishes what he/she took, then more food can be taken (just one or two tablespoon at a time).

The traditional way of eating Thai style (central Thai) is that diners have their own plates of rice and share several dishes (กับข้าว) that are placed in the middle in front of all diners. Dishes served are different in flavor and texture: some spicy, some mild, some tangy, some soft, some crunchy, etc. Diners take one or two tablespoon-fuls of one dish to eat with their rice. After finishing what they take, they can take more of whatever suits their taste (i.e. they might want to choose a milder dish if the first dish is a little too spicy, in order to cool off the palate).

Thais use forks and spoons when eating rice, unless rice is served in a bowl or as rice soup. Chopsticks are used with food that comes in bowls but not on plates (e.g. ผัดไทย is served with fork and spoon, not chopsticks). Eating with hands is appropriate with certain types of food, e.g. ข้าวเหนียว and ไก่ย่าง.

Rice is the main staple for Thai people and is considered "holy." Thai children are taught to be grateful to rice and to pay respect to it as there is แม่โพสพ (the Rice Goddess) in every grain of rice! Some children will ไหว้ after the end of the meal to express thanks to the Rice Goddess!

Unit 6
Getting around Town

Lesson 23: Asking for Location

 คำศัพท์

PREPOSITIONS

บน	on	(ข้าง)นอก	outside
ใต้	under	ติดกับ	next to
ตรงข้าม	opposite	ระหว่าง	between
ข้าง	side, beside	มุม/หัวมุม	in the corner
ข้างหน้า	in front, ahead	ไกล	far
ข้างหลัง	behind, in back	ใกล้	near
ข้างซ้าย/ซ้ายมือ	to the left/ left hand	ข้างบน	on top
ข้างขวา/ขวามือ	to the right/right hand	ข้างล่าง	beneath
(ข้าง)ใน	inside	เหนือ	above

NOUNS

ห้อง (ห้อง)	room	หน้าต่าง (บาน)	window
ประตู (บาน)	door	ชั้น	level, floor
เก้าอี้ (ตัว)	chair		

แผนกสอบถาม	information desk	โรงอาหาร (โรง)	cafeteria
ห้องสมุด (แห่ง)	library	ร้านกาแฟ (ร้าน)	coffee shop
ร้านหนังสือ (ร้าน)	bookstore	สนามบิน (แห่ง)	airport
ไปรษณีย์ (แห่ง)	post office	สถานีรถไฟ (สถานี)	train station
มหาวิทยาลัย (มหาวิทยาลัย)	university	ปั๊มน้ำมัน (ปั๊ม)	gas station
ศูนย์การค้า (แห่ง)	shopping center	วัด (วัด)	temple
โรงหนัง (โรง)	movie theater	ร้าน(ขาย)ของเล่น (ร้าน)	toy store
ร้านดอกไม้ (ร้าน)	flower shop	ที่ทำงาน	office

ห้องรับแขก (ห้อง)	living room	ห้องน้ำ (ห้อง)	bathroom
ห้องกินข้าว (ห้อง)	dining room	ห้องส้วม (ห้อง)	toilet
ห้องนั่งเล่น (ห้อง)	family room	ห้องทำงาน (ห้อง)	den, office
ห้องนอน (ห้อง)	bedroom	ชั้นบน/ข้างบน	upstairs
ห้องครัว (ห้อง)	kitchen	ชั้นล่าง/ข้างล่าง	downstairs

*Words in parentheses are classifiers.

VERBS

คิด	to think
เข้าใจ	to understand
หาเจอ/หาไม่เจอ	able/unable to find something
รู้/ทราบ	to know (information)
แน่ใจ	to be certain
บอก	to tell, to say
ถาม	to ask

MISC.

แบบ	kind, type

PATTERNS

หนังสืออยู่ที่ไหน	Where is the book?
หนังสืออยู่บนโต๊ะ	It's on the table.
” ใต้โต๊ะ	It's under the table.
” ข้างๆ โต๊ะ	It's next to the table.
” (ข้าง)นอกห้อง	It's outside the room.
” (ข้าง)ในห้อง	It is inside the room.

หนังสืออยู่ตรงไหน ดิฉัน/ผมหาไม่เจอ	Where (exactly) is the book? I can't find it.
อยู่ระหว่างโต๊ะกับเก้าอี้	(It's) between the desk and the chair.
อยู่ตรงมุมห้อง	It is at the corner of the room.
อยู่นี่เอง (หา)เจอแล้ว	Here it is. I found it.

ทอมนั่งตรงไหน	Where (exactly) does Tom sit?
ระหว่างเจนกับซูซาน	(He's) between Jane and Susan.
ข้างๆ ซูซาน	(He's) beside Susan.

คุณรู้ไหมว่าไปรษณีย์อยู่ที่ไหน   Do you know where the post office is?

   (ไปรษณีย์)อยู่ข้างหลังโรงเรียน   (It) is behind a school.

   อยู่ตรงข้ามร้านอาหาร   (It) is opposite a restaurant.

   อยู่ติดกับธนาคาร   (It) is next to a bank.

ห้องรับแขกอยู่ชั้นล่าง แต่ห้องนอนอยู่ชั้นบน

The living room is downstairs but the bedroom is upstairs.

มีห้องน้ำอยู่ในห้องนอนไหม   Is there a bathroom attached to/with the bedroom?

   มีค่ะ/ครับ   Yes, there is.

ห้องน้ำแบบไหน   What type of bathroom?

   ห้องน้ำแบบฝรั่ง   A Western-style bathroom.

ที่ทำงานเขาอยู่ชั้นไหน

On what floor is his office?

ไปถามที่แผนกประชาสัมพันธ์ซิ

Go ask at the information desk.

เขาคิดว่าห้องสมุดอยู่ไม่ไกล

He thinks the library is not far.

แม่บอกลูกว่าหนังสืออยู่บนโต๊ะกินข้าว

Mom told her child that the book is on the dining table.

เขาเข้าใจว่าร้านอาหารอยู่ใกล้ๆ

She understands that the restaurant is very near.

หนังสือของคุณ ถ้าไม่อยู่บนโต๊ะก็อยู่ใต้โต๊ะ

As for your book, if it's not on the table, then it's under the table.

เขาบอกว่า ร้านอาหาร ถ้าไม่อยู่ติดกับธนาคารก็อยู่ใกล้ธนาคาร

He told me that if the restaurant is not next to the bank, then it's close to it.

GRAMMAR

1. คิด, บอก, เข้าใจ, รู้, ทราบ to think, to say/tell, to understand, to know

To say, "I think that.....," "She told me that.....," "I understand that.....,", or "I know that.....," use completive word ว่า in this pattern.

> S + V (คิด/บอก/เข้าใจ/รู้/ทราบ) + ว่า + Sentence or
> Complement Clause

e.g.　เขาคิดว่าคุณพูดภาษาไทยเก่ง

　　　She thinks that you speak Thai well.

　　　ฉันเข้าใจว่าคุณจะไปเมืองไทยปีหน้า

　　　I understand that you will go to Thailand next year.

　　　เขาบอกว่าจะไม่ไปทำงานวันนี้

　　　He said that he would not go to work today.

　　　ฉันรู้ว่าเขาไม่ว่างพรุ่งนี้

　　　I know that she is not free tomorrow.

To say, "He told me that he liked Thai food," use this pattern.

> S + บอก + Pronoun + ว่า + Sentence or Complement Clause

e.g.　ฉันบอกเขาว่าจะไม่ไปทำงานวันนี้

　　　I told her that I would not go to school today.

　　　อาจารย์บอกนักเรียนว่าจะมีสอบพรุ่งนี้

　　　The teacher told the students that there would be a test tomorrow.

　　　เขาบอกฉันว่าคุณมีแฟนแล้ว

　　　She told me that you already had a girlfriend.

DRILL 1

1.　เขาบอกว่าอะไร (อาหาร-เสร็จ)

　　What did he say? (food-done)

　　เขาบอกว่าอาหารเสร็จแล้ว

　　He said that the food was ready.

　　เขาบอกว่าอาหารยังไม่เสร็จ

　　He said that the food was not yet ready.

2.　แม่บอกว่าอะไร (พ่อ-มา)

　　What did Mom say? (Dad-return)

3. คนนั้นบอกว่าอะไร (เขา-หิว)

   What did that person say? (he-hungry)

4. พ่อบอกว่าอะไร (กิน-อิ่ม)

   What did Dad say? (eat-full)

5. ตาบอกว่าอะไร (ยาย-ตื่น)

   What did Grandpa say? (Grandma-up)

6. พี่บอกว่าอะไร (แม่-นอน)

   What did your sister say? (Mom-sleep)

7. ครูบอกว่าอะไร (นักเรียน-กลับ)

   What did the teacher say? (student-back)

8. เพื่อนบอกว่าอะไร (อาหาร-เสีย)

   What did your friend say? (food-spoil)

9. พ่อบอกว่าอะไร (ลูก-กลับ)

   What did the father say? (child-back)

10. พยาบาลบอกว่าอะไร (หมอ-มา)

    What did the nurse say? (doctor-come)

((•)) DRILL 2

1. ไปเมืองไทยได้ไหม (yes)

   Can you go to Thailand?

   ได้ครับ ผมไปเมืองไทยได้ / ได้ค่ะ ดิฉันไปเมืองไทยได้

   Yes, I can go to Thailand.

2. วันอาทิตย์ทำงานได้ไหม (no, busy)

   Can you work on Sundays?

3. ไปดูหนังด้วยกันคืนนี้ได้ไหม (no, too much work)

   Can we go see a movie tonight?

4. กินอาหารเผ็ดได้ไหม (yes, a little bit)

   Can you eat spicy food?

5. เย็นนี้ทำอาหารได้ไหม (no, no time)

   Can you cook this evening?

PARTNER ACTIVITY: มาลีอยู่ที่ไหน

Work in pairs to describe each picture.

CLASS ACTIVITY: TWENTY QUESTIONS

I. Teacher picks a student in the class. Other students ask ใช่ไหม questions to find out who that person is by finding out where he/she is sitting.

II. Students divide up into two teams. After the teacher goes over the vocabulary for items in the classroom, each team picks an object in the classroom for the other team to guess. The team that identifies the object with fewer questions wins (using ใช่ไหม questions, e.g. It is near the door, right?).

III: ไกล, ใกล้

Students divide up into groups of five or six. Each group takes a turn by choosing a person to be blindfolded who is asked to wait outside. The rest of the group picks an object in the classroom and the person waiting outside is let back in blindfolded. The rest of the group has to direct the blindfolded person to the object selected by telling him/her whether or not he/she is hotter or cooler. If he/she is approaching the object, the rest of the group has to tell him "ใกล้." If he/she is straying from the object, the rest of the group has to say "ไกล." Keep giving feedback until he/she reaches the object. The group that uses the least time wins.

GOSSIP GAME

Students divide up into groups of eight and choose a leader. The leader silently reads a secret passage given by the teacher, then whispers the secret to the student sitting next to him or her. The last student tells the class secret. Which group passed on the secret most accurately?

EXERCISES

I. Classifiers: Write ถูก (correct) or ผิด (wrong) in front of these sentences. Rewrite the incorrect sentences.

....	1.	เขามีหนังสือเล่มเดียว
....	2.	คุณมีปากกากี่แท่ง
....	3.	หนังนี้ไม่ยาวเท่าหนังแรก
....	4.	มีคนมากที่ตลาด
....	5.	เขามีกางเกงหลายคู่
....	6.	รถนี้แพงมาก
....	7.	รถของเขาแพงมาก
....	8.	นักเรียนทุกมาโรงเรียน
....	9.	เขาเป็นลูกที่สอง
....	10.	ขอกาแฟเย็น ๓ ใบ

II. Translate these sentences.

1. The school is not very far from my house.

2. My mom told me that the bank is next to a Thai restaurant.

3. My house is between a coffee shop and a grocery store.

4. We like the same color.

5. I know that we were born on the same day.

Lesson 24: Asking for Directions

VERBS

เดิน	to walk	หา	to look for
ขี่	to ride a bicycle or motorcycle	ชี้	to point
เลี้ยว	to turn	ถึง	to arrive, to reach
รู้จัก	to know (person), to be familiar with	ขับรถ	to drive
ผ่าน	to pass	หลงทาง	to be lost

NOUNS

ทาง (ทาง)	way	ซอย (ซอย)	soi, little street
ไฟแดง (ไฟแดง)	traffic light	ถนน (สาย)	street, road
สัญญาจราจร (สัญญาณจราจร)	traffic light	ทางด่วน (สาย)	expressway
		โทล์เวย์ (สาย)	toll way
สี่แยก (สี่แยก)	intersection	แผนที่ (แผ่น)	map
ทางแยก (ทางแยก)	fork	ป้ายรถเมล์ (ป้าย)	bus stop
วงเวียน (วงเวียน)	traffic circle		

(รถ)ตุ๊กๆ, รถสามล้อเครื่อง (คัน)	tuk-tuk
รถเมล์, รถประจำทาง (คัน)	bus
รถป.อ., รถปรับอากาศ (คัน)	air-conditioned bus
รถแท็กซี่ (คัน)	taxi
รถมอเตอร์ไซค์ (คัน)	motorcycle
รถสองแถว (คัน)	two-row bus
บีทีเอส (ขบวน)	BTS (Thai monorail)
เอ็มทีเอส, รถไฟใต้ดิน (ขบวน)	MTS (Thai subway)

*Words in parentheses are classifiers.

MISC.

.....ตรงไป   to.....straight ahead (i.e. เดินตรงไป, ขับรถตรงไป)

จนถึง   until

ซัก/สัก   about

PREPOSITION

โดย   by

PATTERNS

ขอโทษค่ะ/ครับ ช่วยบอกทางหน่อยได้ไหมคะ/ครับ

Excuse me. Could you give me directions?

ช่วยชี้ทางหน่อยได้ไหม

Could you please point me the way?

คุณรู้จักร้านอาหารนิคไหม

Do you know Nick's Restaurant?

คุณรู้ไหมว่าร้านอาหารนิคอยู่ที่ไหน

Do you know where Nick's Restaurant is?

เขาหลงทาง

He's lost.

ไปรษณีย์ไปทางไหน/ไปรษณีย์อยู่ทางไหน/ไปรษณีย์อยู่ตรงไหน

Where is the post office?

    เดินตรงไปทางนี้

    Walk this way.

    ขับรถตรงไปทางนี้

    Drive this way.

    อยู่ทางนี้ เดินตรงไปซัก ๓ ป้ายรถเมล์

    It's this way. Walk straight ahead about three bus stops.

    แล้วเลี้ยวซ้ายที่สี่แยก

    Then turn left at the intersection.

แล้วเลี้ยวขวาที่ไฟแดง
Then turn right at the light.
แล้วเลี้ยวขวาที่มุมถนน
Then turn right at the corner.

เดินตรงไป จนถึง สามแยก แล้วเลี้ยวขวา
Walk straight ahead until the intersection, then turn right.

เดินตรงไป จนถึง สี่แยก แล้ว เลี้ยวซ้าย
Walk straight ahead until the intersection, then turn left.

เดินตรงไป จนถึง ไฟแดง แล้ว เลี้ยวขวา
Walk straight ahead until the traffic light, then turn right.

เดินตรงไปทางนี้ พอถึงสี่แยก ก็ เลี้ยวซ้าย
Walk straight this way. Turn left as soon as you arrive at the intersection.

เดินตรงไปทางนี้ ผ่านไฟแดงแล้วเลี้ยวขวาที่ทางแยก
Walk straight this way. Walk past the traffic light, then turn right at the fork.

ไปรษณีย์อยู่ทางซ้าย
The post office is on the left.

ขับรถไปตามถนนราชดำริ แล้วเลี้ยวซ้ายที่ถนนพระราม ๑
Drive along Rajdamri Road, then turn left at Rama I Road.

ไปรษณีย์อยู่ซ้ายมือ
The post office is on your left.

ไปรษณีย์อยู่ตรงไหน
Where is the post office?
   อยู่ตรงนี้เอง
   It is right here!
   อยู่ตรงโน่น
   It's all the way over there.

ไกลมากไหมคะ/ครับ

Is it very far?

ไม่ไกล เดินไปได้

No, not far. You can walk.

ไกลมาก เดินไปไม่ได้ ต้องขึ้นรถไป

It's very far. You can't walk there. You have to go by car.

ไปรถเมล์เบอร์อะไรได้บ้างคะ/ครับ

Which number bus can I take?

ไปเบอร์ ๔ หรือ เบอร์ ๕๐ ก็ได้

You can take bus number 4 or 50.

ไป บีทีเอส ดีกว่าแท็กซี่

It's better to go by BTS than taxi.

เขาบอกให้ฉันขึ้นรถเมล์เบอร์ ๔

She told me to take bus number 4.

เขาบอกให้ฉันเลี้ยวซ้ายที่สี่แยก

She told me to turn left at the intersection.

เขานั่งรถเมล์มาโรงเรียน

He took a bus to school.

เขามาโรงเรียนโดยทางรถเมล์

He came to school by bus.

GRAMMAR

1. **บอกให้** to tell someone to do something

To say, "Mom told me to do my homework," or "He told me to speak louder," use the patterns below.

> S + บอกให้ + Pronoun + VP
>
> or
>
> S + บอก + Pronoun + ให้ + VP

e.g. แม่บอกฉันให้ล้างจาน   Mom told me to do the dishes.

แม่บอกให้ฉันไปนอน   Mom told me to go to bed.

อาจารย์บอกให้นักเรียนพูดตาม   Teacher told the students to repeat after (her).

DRILL

1. เขาทำงานตรงนี้ใช่ไหม (no, over there)

   She works right here, right?

   ไม่ใช่ เขาทำงานตรงนั้น

2. ไปรษณีย์อยู่ตรงนั้นใช่ไหม (no, over here)

   The post office is over there, right?

3. ธนาคารอยู่ข้างซ้ายของไปรษณีย์ใช่ไหม (no, to the right)

   The bank is on the left of the post office, right?

4. เลี้ยวขวาตรงสี่แยกใช่ไหม (no, at the traffic light)

   Turn right at the intersection, right?

5. เลี้ยวขวาตรงไฟแดงใช่ไหม (no, turn left)

   Turn right at the traffic light, right?

6. บ้านเพื่อนอยู่ใกล้ตลาดใช่ไหม (no, close to a hotel)

   Your friend's house is close to the market, right?

7. ร้านอาหารอยู่ในตลาดใช่ไหม (no, it's between a hotel and a bank)

   The restaurant is in the market, right?

8. บ้านเพื่อนอยู่ทางนี้ใช่ไหม (no, it's that way)

   Your friend's house is this way, right?

SUBSTITUTION DRILL

เดิน	ตรงไป	จนถึง	สามแยก	แล้ว	เลี้ยว	ขวา
ขับรถ						
			ไฟแดง			
						ซ้าย
			มุมถนน			
			ซอยข้างหน้า			
เดิน						
						ขวา

CLASS ACTIVITY

Using the map below, ask students to give the following directions:

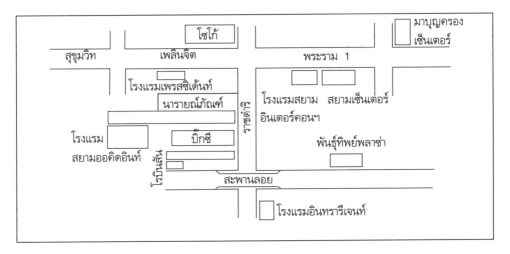

1. From President Hotel to Mabunkhrong Center;
2. From Mabunkhrong Center (MBK) to Phanthip Plaza;
3. From Phanthip Plaza to Siam Intercontinental Hotel;
4. From Siam Intercontinental to Siam Orchid Inn Hotel;
5. From Siam Orchid Inn Hotel to Siam Center.

EXERCISES

I. Rearrange the dialogue below.

.... เดินไปทางไหนคะ

.... ไม่เป็นไรค่ะ

.... ธนาคารอยู่ทางซ้ายมือหรือขวามือคะ

.... เลี้ยวขวาแล้วเดินไปอีกไกลไหม

.... ขอโทษค่ะ คุณรู้ไหมว่าธนาคารกรุงเทพอยู่ที่ไหน

.... อยู่ติดกับไปรษณีย์ ไม่ไกลหรอก เดินไปได้

.... ไม่ไกลหรอก เดินไปนิดเดียวก็ถึง

.... อยู่ขวามือค่ะ อยู่ติดกับร้านก๋วยเตี๋ยว

.... เดินตรงไปทางนี้ จนถึงสี่แยก แล้วเลี้ยวขวา

.... ขอบคุณมากค่ะ

II. Translate these sentences into Thai.

1. How much are these shoes? This pair is 300 baht; that one is 400 baht.

2. Mother had her son go buy groceries for her. He bought two chickens and four oranges.

3. Can you speak and read English? Do you know Thai? I know a little bit.

4. This table is not as big as that one.

5. Is your bedroom upstairs? No, it's downstairs.

6. Excuse me! Do you know the Erawan Hotel?

7. Could you please give me directions to the Erawan Hotel?

8. Walk this way until the intersection. Turn right there.

CULTURAL CORNER

Thais are not trained to read maps. Instead of using east, west, north, south when giving directions, they will use landmarks. Normally, Thais do not give very clear instructions/directions. They tend to point you in the general direction. So it is likely that you will have to ask several people before you reach your destination!

Lesson 25: Transportation

VERBS

ลึก	to be deep	ไปรับ/มารับ	to pick up someone
ตาม	to follow		
ขึ้น	to get on	เข้า	to enter
ลง	to get out/off	จอด	to park
หยุด	to stop	พา...ไป/มา	to take
เลย	to pass, to go beyond		
ย้อนกลับ	to go back, to u-turn		
ไปส่ง/มาส่ง	to drop off someone		
เช่า	to rent	วาง	to place, put down
คืน	to return	จ่าย	to pay
มัดจำ	to leave a deposit		

NOUNS

ที่อยู่/บ้านเลขที่	address
ค่าเช่า	rent (money)
ค่ามัดจำ	deposit
ใบขับขี่ (ใบ)	driver's license
หนังสือเดินทาง (เล่ม)	passport
ใบขับขี่ระหว่างประเทศ (ใบ)	international driver's license
รถโดยสาร (คัน)	passenger vehicle
ผู้โดยสาร (คน)	passenger
ฝั่ง	side (of a street)

*Words in parentheses are classifiers.

PATTERNS: RIDING TUK-TUK, TAXI, AND MOTORCYCLE

ไปไหนครับ	Where do you want to go?
ไปสุขุมวิทซอยร้อยหนึ่ง เท่าไรครับ	To Sukhumvit 101. How much is it?
เข้าซอยไปลึกไหม	Is it deep in the *soi*?
ไม่ลึก นิดเดียวก็ถึง	No, it's not.
หนึ่งร้อย/ร้อยนึงครับ	100 baht.
แปดสิบก็แล้วกัน ผมไปแปดสิบทุกครั้ง/ที	Let's make it 80! I always go for 80 baht.
ไม่ไหว/ไม่ได้ครับ เก้าสิบบาทเถอะ	No, I can't. How about 90 baht?
ตอนนี้รถติดมาก ไม่ไปครับ	The traffic is very congested. I'm not going.
ไปไม่ไหวครับ รถติดมาก	I can't go. The traffic is very bad.
ไปไม่ทันครับ ต้องส่งรถ	I must return the car. I won't be back in time.
นี่ที่อยู่โรงแรม	Here is the hotel address.

Note: Taxis are equipped with meters so bargaining is unusual.

PATTERNS: DRIVING INSTRUCTIONS

ช่วยขับช้าๆ หน่อย	Please slow down.
ขับช้าๆ หน่อยได้ไหม	Could you please slow down?
เข้าซอยข้างหน้า	Go in the *soi* in front.
ตามรถคันหน้าไป	Follow the car ahead.
จะลงตรงไหน	Where do you want to get off?
ไปอีก	Keep going.
ไปอีกหน่อย	Go a little further.
ยังไม่ถึง	We are not there yet.
เลยไปอีกหน่อย	Go a little bit beyond/more.
เลยป้ายรถเมล์ไปหน่อย	Just a little beyond the bus stop.
ถึงแล้ว	We're there.

210

จอดที่นี่	Stop here.
จอดตรงนี้ก็ได้	You can stop here.
จอดตรงนี้ละ	Just stop here.
ช่วยจอดป้ายหน้าด้วย	Please stop at the next bus stop.
ลงฝั่งนี้ก็ได้	I'll get off on this side of the street.
เลยไปแล้ว ช่วยย้อนกลับหน่อย	(We) passed it already. Please go back/U-turn.

PATTERNS: ASKING FOR A RIDE

ช่วยไปส่งถนนสีลมได้ไหม	Could you please drop me off at Silom Rd.?
ช่วยไปส่งที่สนามบินดอนเมืองได้ไหม	Could you please drive me to/drop me off at Don Muang airport?
ช่วยพาไปโรงพยาบาลหน่อยได้ไหม	Could you please take me to the hospital?
ช่วยพาฉันไปหาหมอหน่อยได้ไหม	Could you take me to see a doctor?
ช่วยมารับฉันที่สนามบินได้ไหม	Could you please pick me up at the airport?
ช่วยมารับฉันตอนบ่ายสามโมงด้วยนะ	Please pick me up at three p.m., O.K.?

211

PATTERNS: RENTING A VEHICLE

อยากเช่ารถมอเตอร์ไซค์	I would like to rent a motorcycle.
ค่าเช่าวันละเท่าไร	What is the rate per day?
เอากี่วัน	How many days do you want it for?
สามวัน	Three days.
ต้องคืนรถก่อนเที่ยงนะ	You must turn it in before noon.
ช่วยวางมัดจำด้วย	Please leave a deposit.
ค่ามัดจำเท่าไร	How much is the deposit?
จ่ายค่าเช่าด้วย	Please pay the rent.
ขอหนังสือเดินทางด้วย	May I have your passport?
ขอใบขับขี่ด้วย	May I have your driver's license?

GRAMMAR

1. อีก more, again

To say, "I want to eat more," or "I want to order two more plates of *phat thai*," or "I want to see you again," use the patterns below.

> S + VP + อีก
>
> S + V + DO (noun) + อีก + number + Clf.

e.g.	เขาอยากไปเมืองไทยอีก	He would like to go to Thailand again.
	ฉันอยากกินอีก ยังไม่อิ่ม	I would like to eat more. I'm not full.
	อยากสั่งอาหารอีกสามอย่าง	(I) would like to order three more dishes.
	พี่สาวซื้อเสื้ออีกสามตัว	My older sister bought three more blouses.
	ขออีกหน่อย	May I have a little bit more?

2. ค่า prefix for fee, cost, price, value

Place prefix ค่า in front of a verb or a noun to create new compound words.

e.g. ค่ากิน   cost of food, food expense

ค่ากินอยู่   living expense

ค่าดู   admission fee (to a theater, etc)

ค่ารถ   fare

ค่าน้ำค่าไฟ   cost of utilities

ค่าโทรศัพท์   telephone bill

ค่าตั๋ว   ticket price

3. พา.....ไป/มา to bring, to take

To say, "I take my friends to Thailand," or "She brought her children to see her parents," use **พา** in the patterns below.

> S + พา + Someone + ไป/มา + Somewhere
>
> S + พา + Someone + ไปหา/มาหา + Someone

e.g. เขาพาลูกๆ ไปดูหนัง   She took her children to see a movie.

เขาพาลูกๆ ไปหาหมอ   She took her children to see a doctor.

 DRILL

1. เขาขับรถเป็นไหม (no, because he has never driven before)

   Can he drive?

   ไม่เป็นเพราะเขาไม่เคยขับรถมาก่อน

2. เขาพูดภาษาเยอรมันได้ไหม (no, but he can speak French)

   Can he speak German?

3. เขาเดินไหวไหม (no, because he is very tired)

   Can he walk?

4. ที่นี่อาหารเผ็ดมาก เขากินได้ไหม (no, because it's too spicy)

   The food is very spicy here. Can he eat it?

5. วันนี้เขาไปโรงเรียนไหวไหม (no, he is still sick)

   Can he go to school today?

6. คุณทำอาหารให้เราได้ไหม (no, I don't know how)

   Can you cook for us?

7. ช่วยขับรถไปส่งหน่อยได้ไหม (no, I don't have a car)

   Could you please drive me (somewhere)?

8. ช่วยมารับฉันหน่อยได้ไหม (no, I have to work)

   Could you please pick me up?

EXERCISES

I. How do you say this in Thai?

1. Slow down please.

2. Turn right at this *soi*.

3. Could you please drive me to the airport?

4. Could you please pick me up here at 3:30 p.m.?

5. How much is the rent per month?

6. Do I have to leave a deposit?

II. Complete the dialogue below.

On Thanon Sukhumvit:

ก: ขอโทษนะคะ คุณรู้จักร้านอาหารบ้านไทยไหมคะ

ข: ....

ก: ช่วยบอกทางหน่อยได้ไหม

ข: ....

ก: คุณจำได้ไหมคะว่าธนาคารชื่ออะไร

ข: ....

ก: ไกลไหมคะ เดินไปซักกี่ป้าย (ซัก = just about)

ข: ....

ก: ไปเบอร์อะไรได้บ้างคะ

ข: ....

ก: ขอบคุณมากค่ะ

ข: ....

Unit 7
Running Errands

Lesson 26: On the Telephone

คำศัพท์

VERBS

ติดต่อ	to contact
โทร, โทรศัพท์	to call
โทรไปหา..., โทรมาหา...	to call (someone)
รับโทรศัพท์	to answer the phone
หมุน	to dial (rotary phone)
วางหู, วางสาย	to hang up
ต่อ	to dial, to connect (extension)
กด	to press (touch phone)
ฟังไม่ได้ยิน	cannot hear
เสีย	to be out of order (e.g. telephone, radio, car)

NOUNS

สาย (สาย)	telephone line
ข้อความ (ข้อความ)	message
โอเปอร์เรเตอร์ (คน)	operator
โทรศัพท์ทางไกล	long distance phone call
โทรศัพท์มือถือ (เครื่อง)	mobile phone
ค่าโทรศัพท์	phone bill, phone charge
สมุดโทรศัพท์ (เล่ม)	phone book
เบอร์โทรศัพท์ (เบอร์)	telephone number
โทรศัพท์สาธารณะ (เครื่อง)	public phone
รหัสพื้นที่ (รหัส)	area code

*Words in parentheses are classifiers.

 PATTERNS

ขอใช้โทรศัพท์ได้ไหมคะ/ครับ	May I use your phone?
ขอเรียนสาย(คุณ)มาลีค่ะ/ครับ	May I speak to Malee? (more formal)
ขอสายคุณมาลีหน่อยค่ะ/ครับ	May I speak to Malee? (formal)
คอยเดี๋ยวนะคะ/ครับ	Wait a moment, please.
สักครู่ค่ะ/ครับ	One moment, please.
รอเดี๋ยวนะคะ/ครับ	Wait a moment, please.
เดี๋ยวค่ะ/ครับ	One moment, please.
ไม่อยู่ค่ะ/ครับ ออกไปแล้ว	She is not here. She's already left.
ขอพูดกับคุณมาลีค่ะ/ครับ	May I speak to Malee?
กำลังพูดค่ะ	Speaking.
ฮัลโหล นี่มาลีค่ะ	Hello. This is Malee speaking.
ขอโทษ คุณมีเบอร์ (ของ) มาลีมั้ย	Excuse me. Do you have Malee's number?
ไม่มีค่ะ/ครับ คุณต้องโทรไปถาม ๑๘๓	No, I don't. You have to call 183.
ช่วย (กรุณา) ต่อเบอร์ ๒๓๔ หน่อยค่ะ/ครับ	Please connect me to extension 234.
ที่นี่ไม่มีคนชื่อมาลีค่ะ/ครับ	There is no one here named Malee.
ขอโทษ ต่อ(เบอร์) ผิดค่ะ/ครับ	Excuse me. I dialed the wrong number.

ขอฝากข้อความหน่อยได้ไหมคะ/ครับ	May I leave a message? (polite)
สั่งอะไรไว้ได้มั้ยคะ/ครับ	May I leave a message?
จะสั่งอะไรถึงคุณมาลีมั้ย	Would you like to leave a message for Malee?
ช่วยบอกคุณมาลีว่านิดโทรมา	Please tell Malee that Nid called.
ช่วยบอกให้เขาโทรกลับมาด้วยนะคะ/ครับ	Please tell her to call me back.
ดิฉัน/ผมติดต่อเขาไม่ได้	I can't contact him.
โทรศัพท์สายไม่ว่าง	The line is busy.
ไม่มีคนรับสาย	No one answers.
ต่อไม่ติด	There was no connection.
โทรไม่ได้ สายเสีย	You can't call. The line is out of order/dead.
(ฟัง)ไม่ได้ยินค่ะ/ครับ สายไม่ค่อยดี ช่วยพูดดังๆ หน่อยค่ะ/ครับ	I can't hear you. The connection is bad. Please speak louder.
กรุณาโทรมาใหม่นะคะ/ครับ	Please call back (later).
จะโทรกลับไปเมื่อไรดีคะ/ครับ	When is a good time to call back?
ช่วยต่ออีกทีค่ะ/ครับ สายตก	Please connect me again. The line was cut.
ช่วยต่อเบอร์นี้ให้หน่อยได้ไหม	Would you dial this number for me?
ต้องต่อเบอร์อะไรก่อน	What number do I have to dial first?
พอแค่นี้ก่อนนะคะ/ครับ แค่นี้นะ / แล้วคุยกันใหม่	That's it for now. We'll talk again.

GRAMMAR

Can/Can't expressions

There are some verbs in Thai that require different words rather than ได้ or ไม่ได้ to express ability or inability to do something. For example:

นอน/หลับ

เมื่อคืนนี้เขา**นอนหลับ**สบายมาก

Last night he slept so well.

เขาคิดมากเลย**นอนไม่หลับ**

He worried too much, so he couldn't sleep.

เขากินกาแฟมากเลย**นอนไม่หลับ**

He drank too much coffee so he couldn't sleep.

อ่าน/ออก

คุณ**อ่าน**จดหมายฉบับนี้**ออก**ไหม

Can you read this letter?

เขา**อ่าน**ภาษาจีน**ไม่ออก**เพราะเขาไม่เคยเรียน

I can't read Chinese because I have never studied it.

เขาเขียนตัวเล็กมาก เลย**อ่านไม่ออก**

She wrote in such small print that I couldn't read it.

ฟัง/ได้ยิน

พูดดังๆ หน่อย ฉัน**ฟังไม่ได้ยิน**เลย

Please speak louder. I can't hear.

เปิด/ออก

ฉัน**เปิด**ขวด**ไม่ออก** ช่วยหน่อยได้ไหม

I can't open this bottle. Can you help me?

เขาล็อคประตูแล้ว **เปิดไม่ออก**หรอก

She already locked the door. You can't open it.

มอง/เห็น

คุณเขียนตัวเล็กจัง ฉัน**มองไม่เห็น**

You wrote too small; I can't see it.

เขาอยู่ไหน ฉัน**มองไม่เห็น**

Where is he? I can't see him.

คิด/ออก

ฉัน**คิดออก**แล้วว่าเคยเจอเขาที่ไหน

I can recall now where I met her before.

เธอคิดเลขข้อนี้**ออก**ไหม

Can you solve this math problem?

เขาชื่ออะไรนะ ฉัน**คิดไม่ออก**

What is her name? I can't recall.

นึก/ออก

ฉัน**นึกออก**แล้วว่าฉันเคยเจอเขาที่ไหน

I can recall now where I met him before.

ฉัน**นึก**ชื่อเขา**ไม่ออก** เธอจำชื่อเขาได้มั้ย

I can't think of his name. Do you remember?

กิน/ลง

ร้านนี้ทำอาหารไม่อร่อยเลย ฉัน**กินไม่ลง**

This restaurant made such terrible food. I couldn't eat it

เขา**กินไม่ลง**เพราะเขาไม่สบาย

She couldn't eat because he was so sick.

PARTNER ACTIVITIES

I. Role Play I

Student 1:   You are calling your best friend. She is not home. Ask when is she going to return home and if she can call you back today.

Student 2:   You are answering a call for your son who is not home at the moment. You know that he went to the library but you do not know when he is going to be home. Ask the caller if he wants to leave a message. (Variation: Student 2 can be a servant answering the phone.)

II. Role Play II

Student 1:   You are calling your professor to make an appointment with him/her. You ask an operator to make a connection for you (by giving him/her the exten-sion number). His/her secretary answers the phone. Ask him/her if you can talk to your professor.

Student 2:   You are a secretary at Chulalongkorn University. Someone calls for Professor.........who is in a meeting. Ask him/her to call back in an hour.

III. Role Play III

Student 1 :   You are calling a friend to invite him/her for lunch and a movie. Pick a date, time, and place.

Student 2 :   You are answering a phone call from a friend. You have a very busy schedule this week (test, job, etc.). You are trying to squeeze in a date with your close friend. You have only three hours to spare so you have to choose what to do!!

WRITING EXERCISES

I. Write down one of the above conversations/dialogues and turn it in to the teacher.

II. Work with your partner. Complete these sentences.

1.   วันนี้เขาไม่ค่อยสบาย   เพราะ เมื่อคืนนี้เขานอน...............
2.   ฉันคิด...............ว่าวางกุญแจรถไว้ที่ไหน   (กุญแจ keys)
3.   คุณต้องพูดอีกที เพราะเขาฟัง...............
4.   ฉันหิวอีกแล้ว เพราะเมื่อกี้นี้กิน...............
5.   เธออ่านลายมือฉัน...............มั้ย (ลายมือ = handwriting)
6.   นี่ภาษาอะไร ฉันอ่าน...............
7.   ร้านนี้ทำอาหารไม่น่ากินเลย ฉันกิน...............หรอก
8.   ช่วยฉันหน่อย ฉันเปิดขวดกาแฟ...............
9.   เสียงดังอย่างนี้ ฉันนอน...............หรอก
10. หนังสืออยู่ตรงนั้นเอง: "อยู่ตรงไหน ฉันมอง..............."

Lesson 27: Finding a Place to Stay

🔊 คำศัพท์

VERBS

สำรอง	to reserve
เงียบ	to be quiet
เปลี่ยน	to change
พร้อม	to be ready, to be equipped with
เต็ม	to be full
ธรรมดา	to be regular, to be normal
ฝาก	to entrust, to leave something to be in someone's care
สกปรก	to be dirty
รวม	to include
ดับ	to extinguish
ไหล	to flow
ดัง	to be loud

NOUNS

แบบ (แบบ)	kind, style	เตียงคู่ (เตียง)	double bed
พัดลม (เครื่อง)	electric fan	เตียงเดี่ยว (เตียง)	twin bed
กุญแจ (ดอก)	keys	ตู้เสื้อผ้า (ตู้)	dresser
ยุง (ตัว)	mosquitoes	หมอน (ใบ)	pillow
ไฟ(ฟ้า)	light, electricity	ปลอกหมอน (ใบ)	pillowcase
อพาร์ต์เมนท์ (หลัง)	apartment	ผ้าปูเตียง (ผืน)	sheet
ห้องเช่า (ห้อง)	room for rent	ผ้าห่ม (ผืน)	blanket
แฟลต (หลัง)	flat	โต๊ะเขียนหนังสือ (ตัว)	desk
เจ้าของบ้าน (คน)	landlord	โซฟา (ตัว)	sofa
บริเวณ/แถว	area, vicinity	ของ (ชิ้น)	thing
เฟอร์นิเจอร์ (ชิ้น)	furniture	เสียง	noise, voice

*Words in parentheses are classifiers.

222

MISC.

แต่.....เท่านั้น	only	อีก	more
มี	there is, there are	ต่างหาก	separately

🔊 PATTERNS: RENTING AN APARTMENT

แถวนี้มีห้องว่างให้เช่าไหมคะ/ครับ	Is there room for rent around here?
มีห้องว่างให้เช่า	(There are) rooms for rent.
บ้านเช่าสามห้องนอน หนึ่งห้องน้ำ	Three bedrooms and one bath rental house.
มีห้องพักหนึ่งห้องนอนว่างไหม	Is there a one bedroom unit available?
จะเช่าเป็นเดือน หรือเป็นปี	Do you want to rent on a monthly or yearly basis?

มีเฟอร์นิเจอร์ไหม	Is there furniture?
มีเฟอร์นิเจอร์พร้อม	The room is furnished.
ไม่มี ต้องหามาเอง	No, you have to furnish it yourself.

ค่าเช่าเดือนละเท่าไร	How much is the rent per month?
รวมค่าน้ำ ค่าไฟมั้ย	Does it include water and the electric bills?
ไม่ค่ะ/ครับ ค่าน้ำค่าไฟต่างหาก	No. Water and electric bills are separate.
มีคนทำความสะอาดมั้ย	Is a cleaning service included? / Is there a cleaning person?
ตามปกติ ค่าไฟราวๆ เดือนละ เท่าไร	Normally, how much is the electric bill, approximately?

PATTERNS: RENTING A ROOM IN A HOTEL

มีห้องว่างมั้ย	Are there any rooms available?
มีครับ ต้องการห้องแบบไหน	Yes. What kind (of room) do you want?
ไม่มีครับ เต็มหมด	No. We are full.
จองห้องไว้ได้มั้ย	May I reserve a room?
ได้ค่ะ/ครับ จะมาวันไหน	Yes. What day are you coming?
มีห้องแอร์มั้ย	Do you have air-conditioned rooms?
ห้องแอร์เต็มหมดแล้ว มีแต่	The air-conditioned rooms are all full.
ห้องธรรมดา(เท่านั้น)	There are only regular rooms left.
ห้องธรรมดามีพัดลมหรือเปล่า	Do regular rooms have fans?
คืนละเท่าไร	How much is it for a night?
มีห้องถูกกว่านี้หรือเปล่า	Are there any cheaper rooms?
จะอยู่กี่คืน	How many nights are you going to stay?
จะอยู่อีกกี่คืน	How many more nights will you stay?
ถ้าอยู่นานจะได้ลดมั้ย	If I stay long, will I get a discount?
ขอดูห้องก่อนได้มั้ย	May I see the room first?
อยากได้ห้องเงียบๆ ชั้นบน	I would like a quiet room upstairs.
ขอห้องเงียบๆ นะ	May I have a quiet room, please?
ขอห้องที่มีวิวนะคะ/ครับ	May I have a room with a view?
ขอเปลี่ยนห้องได้มั้ย	May I change rooms?
จะเช็คเอาท์วันนี้	I'm checking out today.

เวลาเช็คเอาท์กี่โมง	What is the check-out time?
ขอเช็คเอาท์หลังเที่ยงได้มั้ย	Can I check-out after noontime?
นี่ค่ะ/ครับกุญแจ ห้องเบอร์ ๒๐๓	Here is the key. Room number 203.
ฝากของหน่อยได้มั้ย	May I leave my things here?
ฝากกระเป๋าหน่อยได้มั้ย	May I leave my luggage here?
แถวนี้มีธนาคารมั้ย	Is there a bank in this area?
ขอหมอนเพิ่มหนึ่งใบ	May I have one more pillow?
ยุงเยอะ	There are a lot of mosquitos!
ไฟดับ	There is no electricity.
น้ำไม่ไหล	There is no water (water is not running).
โรงแรมนี้น่าอยู่มั้ย	Is this hotel a nice place to stay?
ไม่น่าอยู่เลย สกปรกและเสียงดัง	No, it isn't. It is dirty and noisy.

GRAMMAR

1. แต่.....เท่านั้น only

To say, "I have only sisters (no brothers)," or "This restaurant sells only Thai food,"
use this pattern.

$$S + V + \quad แต่ \quad + Noun + (เท่านั้น)$$

e.g. เขามีแต่พี่สาวไม่มีน้องสาว

He has only older sisters, not younger sisters.

ร้านนี้ขายแต่อาหารลาวไม่ได้ขายอาหารไทย

This restaurant sells only Lao food, not Thai.

นักเรียนคนนี้ชอบเรียนแต่ภาษา ไม่ชอบเรียนวิชาอื่น

This student likes to learn only languages, not other subjects.

To form a negative sentence using แต่ (only) to correct a misunderstanding, use ไม่ได้ + verb instead of ไม่ + verb.

e.g. เขาไม่ได้มีแต่พี่สาว เขามีพี่ชายด้วย

He not only has an older sister, he also has an older brother.

ร้านนี้ไม่ได้ขายแต่อาหารไทยเท่านั้น มีอาหารฝรั่งขายด้วย

This restaurant sells not only Thai food, it also has Western food.

นักเรียนคนนี้ไม่ได้ชอบเรียนแต่ภาษา เขาชอบเรียนวิชาอื่นด้วย

This student not only likes to study languages, but she also likes other subjects.

2. มี there is, there are

To say, "There are three persons in this room," or "Is there anybody here who speaks Thai?" use มี at the beginning of the sentences.

e.g. มีนักเรียนหลายคนทำการบ้านไม่เสร็จ

There are several students who haven't finished their homework.

มีใครพูดภาษาไทยได้บ้าง

Is there anybody who speaks Thai?

มีคนเยอะที่นี่

There are a lot of people here.

3. น่า + Verb

To say, "The food is appetizing," or "This story is unbelievable," use this pattern.

S + (ไม่) + น่า + Verb

e.g. ร้านนี้ทำอาหารน่ากินมาก

This restaurant makes very appetizing food.

เขาคิดว่าเมืองไทยน่าสนใจมาก

She thinks Thailand is very interesting.

ร้านนี้ไม่น่าซื้อ เพราะของแพงเกินไป

This shop doesn't deserve patronage because things are too expensive.

คุณบอกว่าภาษาไทยไม่น่าสนใจหรือ

Did you say that Thai is not interesting?

DRILL 1

1. ทำไมเขาถึงไม่ซื้อ (แพง)
   เขาไม่ซื้อเพราะมันแพงเกินไป
2. ทำไมเขาถึงไม่กิน (เผ็ด)
3. ทำไมเขาถึงไม่ชอบอยู่อเมริกา (หนาว)
4. ทำไมเขาถึงไม่ดื่ม (ร้อน)
5. ทำไมเขาถึงไม่ชอบ (เสียงดัง)
6. ทำไมเขาถึงไม่สบาย (เหนื่อย)
7. ทำไมเขาถึงไม่ง่วง (ดื่มกาแฟมาก)
8. ทำไมเขาถึงนอนไม่หลับ (นอนมาก)
9. ทำไมเขาถึงอ่านลายมือคุณไม่ออก (เขียนตัวเล็ก)
10. ทำไมเขาถึงกินไม่ลง (อิ่ม)

DRILL 2

1. เขากินอาหารวันละกี่ครั้ง (สาม)
   เขากินอาหารวันละสามครั้ง
2. เขาชอบออกกำลังกายอาทิตย์ละกี่ครั้ง (สามถึงสี่)
3. เขาไปเที่ยวเมืองไทยปีละกี่ครั้ง (สองครั้ง)
4. เขาดูทีวีวันละกี่ชั่วโมง (สี่)
5. เขาไปเยี่ยมยายเดือนละกี่ครั้ง (สาม)
6. เขาทานอาหารนอกบ้านอาทิตย์ละกี่ครั้ง (สอง)
7. เขาไปอยู่เมืองไทยปีละกี่เดือน (สาม)
8. เขาท่องหนังสือวันละกี่ชั่วโมง (สอง)
9. เขาทานข้าวครั้งละกี่จาน (สาม)
10. เขาดื่มไวน์วันละกี่แก้ว (หนึ่ง)

DRILL 3

1. นักเรียนอ่านหนังสือกี่เล่ม (สาม)
   นักเรียนอ่านหนังสือคนละสามเล่ม
2. เพื่อนๆ ดูหนังกี่เรื่อง (สอง)
3. ลูกๆ กินขนมกี่ชิ้น (สาม)
4. เด็กๆ เลี้ยงแมวกี่ตัว (สี่)
5. เด็กๆ อยากซื้อขนมกี่ห่อ (สาม)
6. เพื่อนๆ ซื้อเสื้อกี่ตัว (หลาย)
7. พวกเขาสั่งอาหารกี่จาน (สอง)

227

PARTNER ACTIVITIES

I. With your partner, complete this dialogue.

นักท่องเที่ยว:

พนักงานโรงแรม:　มีครับ ต้องการห้องแบบไหนครับ

นักท่องเที่ยว:

พนักงานโรงแรม:　มีห้องว่างชั้น ๓ กับ ชั้น ๑๐ คุณอยากอยู่ชั้นไหนครับ

นักท่องเที่ยว:

พนักงานโรงแรม:　ถ้างั้นเอาห้องชั้น ๑๐ ดีไหมครับ เงียบกว่าชั้น ๓

นักท่องเที่ยว:

พนักงานโรงแรม:　นี่ครับ กุญแจห้องเบอร์ ๑๐๐๓ ครับ

นักท่องเที่ยว:

พนักงานโรงแรม:　ลิฟท์อยู่ตรงข้ามกับคอฟฟี่ช็อป ไปทางนี้แล้วเลี้ยวขวาจะเห็นลิฟท์อยู่
　　　　　　　ข้างหน้าครับ

II. Rearrange this dialogue in the proper order.

.... นักท่องเที่ยว:　　ถ้างั้นจองวันมะรืนไว้ก็แล้วกัน

.... พนักงานโรงแรม:　ครับ จะพักวันไหนบ้างครับ

.... นักท่องเที่ยว:　　ยังไม่ทราบค่ะ ถ้าอยู่นานจะได้ลดมั้ยคะ

.... พนักงานโรงแรม:　จะอยู่กี่วันครับ

.... นักท่องเที่ยว:　　อยากจะขอจองห้องไว้หน่อยค่ะ

.... พนักงานโรงแรม:　พรุ่งนี้เต็มหมดครับ แต่จะมีห้องว่างเยอะวันมะรืน

.... นักท่องเที่ยว:　　ค่าห้องเท่าไรคะ

.... พนักงานโรงแรม:　จะได้ลด ๑๐ เปอร์เซนต์ ถ้าอยู่ตั้งแต่สอง
　　　　　　　　　　อาทิตย์ขึ้นไปครับ

.... นักท่องเที่ยว:　　วันพรุ่งนี้มีห้องว่างมั้ยคะ

.... พนักงานโรงแรม:　วันธรรมดาคืนละ ๒,๐๐๐ บาท
　　　　　　　　　　วันเสาร์อาทิตย์คืนละ ๒,๕๐๐ บาท ครับ

III. Find a different partner. Write a role play, making a phone call to reserve a room in a hotel in Thailand. Then perform it in front of the class.

VOCABULARY REVIEW

If you were going to stay in a hotel in Thailand, what are some things you would look for?

Lesson 28: At the Bus/Train Station

 คำศัพท์

VERBS

ออก	to exit, to leave
อยู่ห่าง	to be far from
ใช้เวลา	to spend time, to take time
ขึ้น	to get on, to take off (plane)
ลง	to get off, to land (plane)

NOUNS

รถทัวร์ (คัน)	tour bus	ตู้นอน (ตู้)	sleeping berth
รถบัส (คัน)	bus (in general)	ตู้เสบียง (ตู้)	dining car
รถไฟ (ขบวน)	train	ชานชาลา (ชานชาลา)	platform,
รถด่วน (ขบวน)	express train		parking space
รถเร็ว (ขบวน)	fast train	ตั๋ว (ใบ)	ticket
เครื่องบิน (ลำ)	airplane	เที่ยวบิน (เที่ยว)	flight
ที่นั่งชั้นหนึ่ง (ที่)	first-class seat	บัตรขึ้นเครื่อง (ใบ)	boarding pass
ที่นั่งชั้นสอง (ที่)	second-class seat	ประตูทางออก (ประตู)	gate
ที่นั่งชั้นสาม (ที่)	third-class seat	ค่าธรรมเนียม	fee
ที่นั่งชั้นประหยัด (ที่)	economy-class seat	ค่าโดยสาร	fare

*Words in parentheses are classifiers.

Bus stations in Bangkok

หมอชิต/ขนส่งหมอชิต	Northern Bus Station
เอกมัย/ขนส่งเอกมัย	Eastern Bus Station
ขนส่งสายใต้	Southern Bus Station

Train station in Bangkok

| สถานีหัวลำโพง | Hualamphong Train Station |

COMPASS DIRECTIONS

ทิศ	compass direction
(ทิศ)เหนือ	north
(ทิศ)ใต้	south
(ทิศ)ตะวันออก	east
(ทิศ)ตะวันตก	west

MISC.

เที่ยว	trip (classifier)
.....ต่อไป	next....., after this
เว้น, ยกเว้น	except

GRAMMAR

ก็มี.....ก็มี.....	both.....and.....

PATTERNS: FOR TRAIN AND BUS

มีรถไปเชียงใหม่กี่โมง	When is there a bus/train to Chiang Mai?
รถเที่ยวต่อไปออกกี่โมง	When does the next bus/train leave?
รถออกกี่โมง	What time does the bus/train leave?
มีรถออกกี่โมงบ้าง	What time are there buses/trains?
ออกทุกๆ ชั่วโมง	There are buses/trains leaving every hour.
๕ โมงเย็นก็มี สองทุ่มก็มี	There is one at five and one at eight.
มีรถเที่ยวเช้ามั้ย (มีรถออกตอนเช้ามั้ย)	Is there a bus/train in the morning?
มีแต่รถเที่ยวบ่าย ไม่มีเที่ยวเช้า	There are only afternoon buses/trains, no morning departures.
ไปเชียงใหม่กี่ชั่วโมง	How many hours is it to Chiang Mai?

ไปเชียงใหม่ใช้เวลากี่ชั่วโมง	How many hours does it take to Chiang Mai?

ไปเชียงใหม่กี่กิโล

How far is it to Chiang Mai? (how many kilometers?)

เชียงใหม่อยู่ห่างจากกรุงเทพกี่กิโล

How far is it from Chiang Mai to Krungthep? (how many kilometers?)

ไปเชียงใหม่อีกกี่กิโล

How much farther is it to Chiang Mai? (how many more kilometers?)

จะไปถึงเชียงใหม่กี่โมง

When will it arrive in Chiang Mai?

รถไปเชียงใหม่จอดที่ไหน

Where does the bus/train to Chiang Mai park/wait?

ขึ้นรถได้ที่ไหน

Where can I get on the bus/train?

ชานชาลาสิบ

Bay/platform number 10.

ขอจองตั๋วไปเชียงใหม่หน่อย	May I reserve a ticket to Chiang Mai?
เที่ยวเดียว หรือ ไปกลับ	One way or round trip?
ตั๋วไปกลับเท่าไร	How much is a round-trip ticket?
ห้าร้อยบาท	Five hundred baht.
แล้วเที่ยวเดียวล่ะ	What about a one-way ticket?
เที่ยวเดียวสามร้อยบาท	Three hundred baht.
งั้นเอาตั๋วไปกลับสองใบ	In that case, I'll take two round-trip tickets.

(((•))) PATTERNS: FOR TRAINS ONLY

รถไปเชียงใหม่ออกวันไหนบ้าง	On which days does the train go to Chiang Mai?
ออกทุกวัน เว้นวันอาทิตย์	(It) goes every day except Sunday.

วันนี้มีรถด่วนไปเชียงใหม่หรือเปล่า	Are there express trains to Chiang Mai today?
มี/ค่ะครับ มีทั้งรถด่วน และรถเร็ว	Yes, there are both express and fast trains.

อยากไปรถที่มีตู้นอน	I would like to take one with a sleeping berth.

ชั้นสองมีตู้นอนมั้ย	Are there sleeping berths on second-class trains?
ไม่มีครับ ถ้าจะเอาตู้นอนต้องไป ชั้นหนึ่ง	No, if you want a sleeping berth, you'll have to take first class.
รถขบวนนี้มีตู้เสบียงไหม	Is there a dining car on this train?

GRAMMAR

1. .....ก็มี .....ก็มี

One can use .....ก็มี .....ก็มี instead of ทั้ง.....และ to say "There are both.....and....."

Noun or Stative verbs + ก็มี

e.g. คนไทยก็มี คนฝรั่งก็มี   There are both Thais and *farang*.

คนดีก็มี คนเลวก็มี   There are both good and bad people.

ถูกก็มี แพงก็มี   There are both expensive and inexpensive ones.

2. ห่าง to be far

To say, "My house is twenty kilometers from the airport," use this pattern.

Place 1 + อยู่ห่างจาก + Place 2 + (ประมาณ/ราว) + # + ไมล์, กิโล, ชั่วโมง, นาที

e.g. เชียงใหม่อยู่ห่างจากกรุงเทพกี่กิโล

บ้านฉันอยู่ห่างจากมหาวิทยาลัยราวๆ ๑๐ ไมล์

บ้านฉันอยู่ห่างจากมหาวิทยาลัยประมาณ ๒๐ นาที

3. ที่ relative clause

Two sentences can be combined by changing one sentence into a relative clause with ที่.

Sentences		Sentences with Relative Clause ที่
นักเรียนไม่มา	นักเรียนชื่อจิม	นักเรียนที่ไม่มาชื่อจิม
อาจารย์สอนภาษาไทย	อาจารย์เป็นคนไทย	อาจารย์ที่สอนภาษาไทยเป็นคนไทย
แม่ให้เสื้อ	เสื้อสีขาว	เสื้อที่แม่ให้สีขาว
เราไปดูหนัง	หนังไม่สนุก	หนังที่เราไปดูไม่สนุก
ผมชอบผู้หญิง	ผู้หญิงชื่อมาลี	ผู้หญิงที่ผมชอบชื่อมาลี
เขาโทรศัพท์ไปหาเพื่อน	เพื่อนไม่อยู่	เพื่อนที่เขาโทรศัพท์ไปหาไม่อยู่
นักเรียนเคยไปเมืองไทย	นักเรียนพูดไทยเก่ง	นักเรียนที่พูดไทยเก่งเคยไปเมืองไทย

PARTNER ACTIVITIES

I. Look at the tickets below. Then answer the following questions.

1. What type of train were the tickets for? (fast train or express train)

2. What was the destination of this trip?

3. When was the departure date?

4. What time did the train depart?

5. What was the arrival time?

6. Were these tickets for first class, second class, or third class?

7. How much was the fare?

8. Why were they different?

II. Complete the dialogue below. Then perform the role play in front of the class.

ผู้โดยสาร:	ตั๋วไปเชียงใหม่วันนี้ มีว่างไหมคะ
พนักงานขายตั๋ว:	....
ผู้โดยสาร:	สองที่ค่ะ
พนักงานขายตั๋ว:	....
ผู้โดยสาร:	ตั๋วไปกลับค่ะ ....
พนักงานขายตั๋ว:	ออกห้าโมงเย็นครับ ....
ผู้โดยสาร:	เอาที่มีชั้นตู้นอน ชั้นสองมีตู้นอนไหมคะ
พนักงานขายตั๋ว:	....
ผู้โดยสาร:	ถ้างั้น เอาตั๋วชั้นหนึ่งค่ะ

EXERCISE

Combine each pair of sentences into one, using a relative clause with **ที่**.

1. เขากินอาหาร อาหารราคาแพง
2. นาฬิกาหาย พ่อซื้อนาฬิกา
3. นักเรียนขยัน นักเรียนเรียนภาษาไทย
4. เขาซื้อบ้าน บ้านใหญ่
5. เขาทำการบ้าน การบ้านยากมาก
6. นักเรียนไปเมืองไทย นักเรียนมีเพื่อนคนไทยหลายคน

Lesson 29: Medical Emergencies

VERBS

ปวด..... ache (put ปวด before the part of the body that aches.)
e.g. ปวดหัว (headache), ปวดท้อง (stomachache), ปวดฟัน (toothache)

เจ็บ..... pain (put เจ็บ before or sometimes after) the part of the body that hurts,)
     e.g. เจ็บตา, เจ็บมือ, เจ็บคอ or มือเจ็บ, ตาเจ็บ, คอเจ็บ

.....หัก broken (put หัก after whatever is broken e.g. ขาหัก, แขนหัก)

รักษา	to treat
ตรวจ	to check
เยี่ยม	to visit
ห้าม	to forbid, prohibit
แพ้	to be allergic to, e.g. แพ้อากาศ, แพ้อาหารทะเล
ไอ	to cough
คัน	to itch
บาด	to cut, e.g. มีดบาดมือ, แก้วบาดเท้า
บาดเจ็บ	to be injured, to get hurt
ได้รับบาดเจ็บ	to be injured, get wounded
ไหม้	to be burned, e.g. ผิวไหม้
เวียนหัว	to be dizzy
เป็นลม	to faint
สลบ / หมดสติ	to be unconscious
หายใจไม่ออก	to be unable to breathe
เป็นฝี	to have a boil/abscess
อาเจียน (polite) / อ้วก	to vomit

อ่อนแอ / ไม่มีแรง	to be weak/ to have no strength
เสียดท้อง	to have heartburn
ค่อยยังชั่ว	to be better, to recover from illnesses
เลว / แย่	to be bad

PRE-VERB

ถูก / โดน	element used in making passive voice

NOUNS

คนไข้/คนเจ็บ (คน)	patient	ห้องฉุกเฉิน (ห้อง)	emergency room
อาการ (อาการ)	symptoms	ใบสั่งยา	prescription
อุบัติเหตุ (อุบัติเหตุ)	accident	ไม้ค้ำยัน	crutch

BODY PARTS

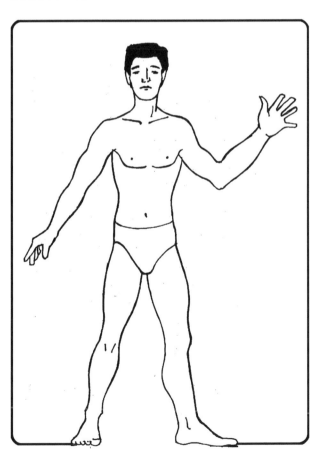

ร่างกาย	body
ศีรษะ, หัว	head
ใบหน้า	face
คิ้ว	eyebrow
แก้ม	cheek
ริมฝีปาก	lip
ลิ้น	tongue
คอ	neck
หน้าอก	chest
หลัง	back
รักแร้	armpit
เอว	waist
ก้น	buttock
หัวเข่า	knee
หน้าผาก	forehead
ตา	eye
จมูก	nose
ปาก	mouth
ฟัน (ซี่)	tooth
คาง	chin
หน้าแข้ง	shin

237

ข้อมือ	wrist	ขา	leg
ฝ่ามือ	palm	น่อง	calf
เท้า	foot	มือ	hand
นิ้วเท้า (นิ้ว)	toe	นิ้ว	finger
ไหล่	shoulder	หู	ear
ท้อง	abdomen	เล็บมือ (เล็บ)	fingernail
แขน	arm	ข้อเท้า	ankle
ข้อศอก	elbow	ผิวหนัง	skin
สะโพก	hip		

*Words in parentheses are classifiers. For body parts that come in pairs, one can specify right or left, this or that, instead of using a classifier, e.g. แขนข้างซ้าย (left arm) or แขนข้างนี้ (this arm).

ILLNESSES

ท้องเสีย	to have diarrhea
ท้องผูก	to have constipation
(มี/เป็น)ไข้	(to have a) fever
(เป็น)หวัด	(to have a) cold
(เป็น)ไข้หวัด	(to have a) cold with fever
(เป็น)ไข้หวัดใหญ่	(to have) flu
(เป็น)ไข้เลือดออก	(to have) dengue fever
(เป็น)มาลาเรีย	(to have) malaria
(เป็น)วัณโรค	(to have) tuberculosis
(เป็น)มะเร็ง	(to have) cancer
อาหารเป็นพิษ	food poisoning

MEDICINE

ยา (เม็ด, หลอด, ขวด)	medicine
กินยา	to take medicine
ยาเม็ด (เม็ด)	pills
ยาน้ำ (ช้อนชา/ช้อนโต๊ะ)	liquid medicine
ยาแก้ไอ	medicine for cough
ยาแก้ปวด	medicine for pain
ยาแก้ไข้	medicine for fever
ยากิน	medicine taken orally

ยาทา	ointment/lotion
ยาอม	lozenge
ยาหม่อง	tiger balm
ฉีดยา	to get an injection (clf. เข็ม e.g. ฉีดยา 2 เข็ม)
ก่อนอาหาร	before meals
หลังอาหาร	after meals
ก่อนเข้านอน	before bed

PATTERNS: USEFUL PHRASES

หายใจเข้า	Breathe in.
หายใจออก	Breathe out.
ถอดเสื้อ	Take off your shirt.
อ้าปาก	Open your mouth.
เลือดกรุ๊ป/กลุ่มอะไร	What is your blood type?
วัดปรอท	to take your temperature
วัดความดัน	to take your blood pressure
ตรวจเลือด	to do a blood exam
ตรวจปัสสาวะ	to do a urine exam
ให้เลือด	to give blood
ให้น้ำเกลือ	to give saline
ถ่ายเอ็กซเรย์	to take an x-ray
ผ่าตัด	to have surgery
ฉีดยาชา	to inject a local anesthetic
วาง/ให้ยาสลบ	to give a general anesthetic
เข้าเฝือก	to have a cast put on
ไม้ค้ำยัน	to use a crutch
แพ้ยา	to be allergic to a medicine, drug

MISC.

V + ขึ้น/ลง	กว่าเดิม, กว่าเก่า
ทันที	immediately

PATTERNS

มีอาการอย่างไรบ้าง	What are your symptoms?
เป็นมาตั้งแต่เมื่อไร	Since when have you had this symptom?
ไม่สบาย อยู่ๆ ก็ปวดหัว	Today I do not feel well. I have a headache all of a sudden.
ไอมาสามวันแล้ว ยังไม่ดีขึ้นเลย	I've had a cough for three days. It is not getting any better.
ตาข้างซ้ายเจ็บ/เจ็บตาข้างซ้าย	My left eye hurts.

ค่อยยังชั่วหรือยัง	Are you better?
วันนี้ดีขึ้น	I feel better today.
วันนี้ค่อยยังชั่ว	Today is better.
ยังไม่ดีขึ้นเลย	It's not getting better.

หายแล้วรึยัง	Have you recovered already? (Are the symptoms all gone?)
หายแล้ว	Yes, they're gone. (I'm fine now).
ยังไม่หาย	No, they're not gone. (I'm still sick).

ทานยาครั้งละ ๒ เม็ด ก่อนอาหารสามเวลา	Take two pills before meals, three times a day.
ทานยาครั้งละ ๑ ช้อนโต๊ะ หลังอาหารและก่อนนอน	Take one tablespoon after meals and before bed.
กินยาให้หมด	Finish all the medicine.
คุณต้องมาเช็คร่างกายอีก	You have to get a check-up again.
ถ้าอาการยังไม่ดีขึ้น ให้มาหาหมออีก	If the conditions have not improved, come see me (doctor) again.

ถ้าอาการเลวลงให้มาหาหมอทันที   If the symptoms/conditions are getting worse, come see me (doctor) right away.

เขาถูก/โดนมีดบาด   He got a cut (from a knife).

มือเขาถูก/โดนไฟไหม้   Her hand got burned.

เขาถูก/โดนรถชน   He got hit by a car.

ห้ามเยี่ยม   Visitation is not allowed/No visitation.

GRAMMAR

1. Passive voice

Passive voice is generally used in Thai *only* when referring to events of violent or unpleasant nature e.g. ถูกต่อย (to be punched), ถูกตี (to be hit), ถูกดุ (to be scolded, to get yelled at), ถูกจับ (to be arrested), ถูกขโมย (to be stolen), ถูกทำโทษ (to be punished). When constructing passive voice, use the pattern below. **โดน** is used instead of **ถูก** in spoken language.

Subject + ถูก/โดน + (Agent) + Verb

e.g.	เขาถูกรถชน	She got hit by a car.
	นักเรียนถูกครูดุ	Students were scolded by the teacher.
	ลูกถูกแม่ตี	A child was spanked by his mother.

In most cases, the passive voice is not used in Thai. There are two choices when dealing with passive voice sentences.

1.1 The sentences are changed into active voice (S + V + O).

e.g.	ทุกคนดูหนังเรื่องนี้แล้ว	This movie was seen by everybody.
	มีคนบอกไม่ให้เขามาที่นี่	He was told not to come here.

1.2 The sentences are written as passive voice but without **ถูก** or **โดน**, relying on the context to make the meaning clear.

e.g.	รถขายไปแล้วเมื่อวานนี้	The car was sold yesterday.
	จดหมายส่งไปแล้ว	The letter was sent already.

2. ขึ้น/ลง

To say, "She is prettier than before," or "The weather is getting worse," use S + V + **ขึ้น/ลง**.

e.g.	เธอสวยขึ้น	She is prettier (than before).

(or เธอสวยกว่าเดิม / เธอสวยกว่าเก่า)

	อากาศเลวลง	The weather is getting worse.

(or อากาศเลวกว่าเดิม, อากาศเลวกว่าเก่า)

ขึ้น is normally used to imply something positive e.g. ดีขึ้น, สวยขึ้น, สูงขึ้น, เก่งขึ้น. **ลง** is used with negative words e.g. เลวลง, แย่ลง, แก่ลง.

PARTNER ACTIVITY

Working with your partner, name various parts of the body.

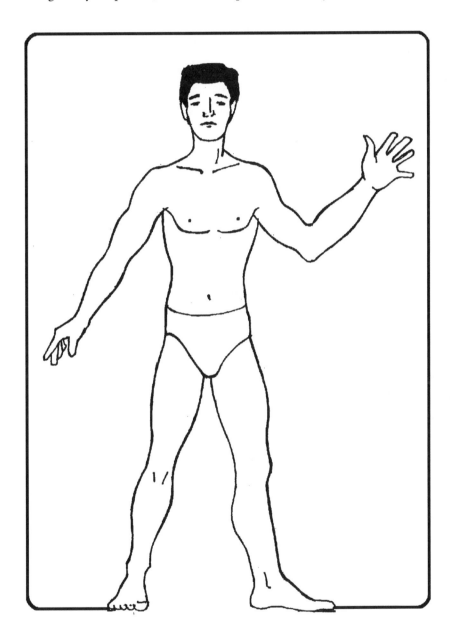

EXERCISES: PASSIVE VOICE

I. Translate these sentences into Thai.

1. This book was written by my teacher.

2. My friend was hit by a car.

3. My car was stolen last week.

4. The letter was sent last week.

5. He was scolded by his father.

6. The book was read by all students.

II. Change these sentences into passive voice.

1. แม่ดุลูก

2. คนนี้ขโมยเงินของผมไป

3. ตำรวจจับขโมยที่หน้าโรงเรียน

4. พ่อตีลูกเพราะลูกดื้อ

5. ครูทำโทษนักเรียนเพราะไม่ทำการบ้าน

Lesson 30: At the Post Office/Bank

 คำศัพท์

NOUNS

ตู้ไปรษณีย์ (ตู้)	mailbox	แสตมป์/ไปรษณียากร (ดวง)	stamp
จดหมาย (ฉบับ)	letter	พัสดุ (ชิ้น,กล่อง)	parcel
ซองจดหมาย (ซอง)	envelope	ค่าประกัน	cost of insurance
จดหมายอากาศ (ฉบับ)	aerogram	ไปรษณียบัตร (ใบ)	postcard
ธนาณัติ (ใบ,ฉบับ)	money order	รหัสไปรษณีย์ (รหัส)	zip code
สมุดเงินฝาก (เล่ม)	bank book	ใบถอนเงิน (ใบ)	withdrawal slip
เช็ค (ใบ,ฉบับ)	check	อัตรา	rate
แบบฟอร์ม (ใบ)	form	แบงค์ (ใบ,ฉบับ)	note
บัญชี (บัญชี)	account	เหรียญ (เหรียญ, อัน)	coin
เช็คเดินทาง (ใบ,ฉบับ)	traveler's check	เศษสตางค์	change (coins)
บัตรเครดิต (ใบ)	credit card	บัตรเอทีเอ็ม (ใบ)	ATM card
ใบฝากเงิน (ใบ)	deposit slip	ตู้เอทีเอ็ม (ตู้)	ATM machine

*Words in parentheses are classifiers.

VERBS

ส่ง	to send	เซ็น	to sign
ส่งโดยด่วน	to send by express	สะสม	to save up, to collect
ลงทะเบียน	to register	ฝาก	to deposit
ประกัน	to insure	กรอก	to fill out a form
ถอน	to withdraw	ขึ้นเงิน	to cash a check
แลก	to exchange		

PATTERNS: AT THE POST OFFICE

ต้องการอะไรคะ/ครับ	What can I do for you?
ขอซื้อแสตมป์ ห้าบาท สิบดวง	I would like to buy ten 5-baht stamps.
แล้วขอจดหมายอากาศ ๔ ฉบับค่ะ/ครับ	And four aerograms, please.

จดหมายอากาศแผ่นละเท่าไรคะ/ครับ

How much does an aerogram cost?

    แผ่นละ ๓๐ บาท

    It's 30 baht for one aerogram.

ส่งจดหมายค่ะ/ครับ

(I would like to) send a letter, please.

    ส่งแบบธรรมดาหรือลงทะเบียน

    Would you like to send it regular mail
    or registered?

ช่วยลงทะเบียนจดหมายฉบับนี้ให้ด้วย

Please register this letter for me.

ค่าส่งเท่าไรคะ/ครับ

How much is the postage?

    ส่งทางเรือ หรือทางอากาศ

    (Would you like to) send it by sea or by
    air?

    ถ้าส่งทางเรือกิโลละ ๕๕๐ บาท ถ้าส่ง
ทางอากาศกิโลละ ๙๑๐ บาท

If sent by sea, it's 550 baht a kilo. If
sent by air, it's 910 baht a kilo.

ส่งทางเรือใช้เวลากี่วัน

How many days does it take by sea?

🔊 PATTERNS: AT THE BANK

ขอถอนเงินหน่อยค่ะ/ครับ	I would like to withdraw money, please.
" ฝาก "	I would like to deposit money, please.
" แลก "	I would like to exchange money, please.
" ขึ้นเงิน "	I would like to cash a check, please.

ขอสมุดเงินฝากหน่อยค่ะ/ครับ

May I have your bank book, please ?

ช่วยกรอกแบบฟอร์มให้หน่อยค่ะ/ครับ

Please fill in the form for me.

ขอแลกเงิน ๑๐๐ ดอลลาร์ค่ะ/ครับ

May I exchange one hundred dollars, please?

ขอดูหนังสือเดินทางด้วยค่ะ/ครับ

May I see your passport, please?

เอาใบละพัน หรือ ใบละห้าร้อยคะ/ครับ

Do you want it in 1,000-baht or 500-baht bills?

ขอ/เอาใบละพัน ๒ ใบ ใบละห้าร้อย ๔ ใบ

May I have two 1,000-baht and four 500-baht bills?

ช่วยเซ็นต์ชื่อตรงนี้ด้วยค่ะ/ครับ

Could you please sign here?

ขอแลกแบงค์พันด้วยค่ะ/ครับ

I would like to change a 1,000 baht bill.

ขอแลกเศษสตางค์ค่ะ

May I change a bill to coins?

ต้องการ/อยากเปิดบัญชีสะสมแบบถอนได้ทุกเวลาค่ะ/ครับ

I'd like to open a savings account that I can withdraw from anytime.

จะเปิดบัญชีเท่าไรคะ/ครับ

How much would you like to deposit (to open the account with)?

สามพันบาทค่ะ/ครับ

Three thousand baht.

GRAMMAR

1. ให้ give

ให้ is a verb but is also used in various expressions which confuse non-native speakers. When using ให้ as a verb, use the pattern below.

S + ให้ + DO + (แก่) + Indirect Object

e.g. แม่ให้เงินลูก   The mother gives money to her children.

ครูให้การบ้านนักเรียน   The teacher gives homework to the students.

พ่อแม่ให้การศึกษาแก่ลูก   Parents give education to their children.

ให้ is also used in various expressions. Study the examples below.

2. ให้ (for) is used when something is done *to* or *for* someone.

e.g. เขาทำอาหารให้แม่   He cooked for his mom.

เขาสอนให้น้องขับรถ   She taught her brother to drive.

พ่อซื้อของให้แม่   Dad bought a gift for Mom.

3. ให้ (so that) in directive sentences indicates result or manner (V + so that + SV).

e.g. ฟังให้ดี	Listen carefully (well).
เขียนให้ถูก	Write correctly.
แต่งตัวให้เรียบร้อย	Dress politely.
กินให้หมด	Eat it all.

4. V + **ให้** means wanting or telling, used with verbs **บอก** (to tell), **อยาก** (to want), **ขอร้อง** (to ask, beg), **สั่ง** (to order).

e.g. ครูอยากให้เราไปเมืองไทย	The teacher wanted us to go to Thailand.
พ่อสั่งให้ลูกทำงานบ้าน	Dad ordered the children to do housework.
เขาขอ(ร้อง)ให้ฉันไปกับเขา	She begged me to go with her.
แม่บอกให้ลูกไปนอน	Mom told the children to go to bed.

5. Expressions with **ให้** mean "to have," "to let."

e.g. พ่อให้ลูกไปดูหนัง	The father let his child see a movie.
ฉันไม่ให้เขาเข้าบ้าน	I didn't let him enter the house.
ครูไม่ให้นักเรียนกลับบ้าน	The teacher didn't let the students go home.

EXERCISES

I. Fill in the blanks.

1.   ....ฉัน..............เขาเรียนภาษาไทย
2.   ฉันเคยไปเมืองไทย..............พี่ชายไม่เคยไป
3.   ฉันชอบอาหารไทย   พี่ชายก็ชอบอาหารไทย..............
4.   พ่อ..............ให้ลูกเรียนภาษาไทย
5.   แม่..............ทำกับข้าว   เราจึงไปกินข้าวนอกบ้านบ่อยๆ
6.   ถ้าคุณไม่สบาย ก็..............ไปหาหมอ
7.   อากาศที่เมืองไทยร้อน..............ที่อเมริกา
8.   คุณชอบเสื้อ..............ไหน
9.   เขาเล่นเปียโน..............เพราะเรียนมาหลายปี
10. คุณทำงาน..............แล้วหรือยัง

II. Translate these phrases with classifiers.

1. some interesting movies

2. two 5-baht stamps

3. every white shirt

4. several kinds of food

5. five times per day

6. which black belt

7. the same house

8. ten long-sleeve shirts

9. how many cars?

10. this Chinese restaurant

WORD INDEX
(indexed by chapter)